Masterpieces in Art

"The Last Prayer —
Christian Martyrs in the Coliseum"

by J. L. Gerome

Written by
William C. Casey

Revised and Edited by
Michael J. McHugh

A PUBLICATION OF
Christian Liberty Press

PREFACE

Simply stated, this text seeks to put within easy reach of teachers and elementary art students a comprehensive study of masterpieces in art. This book is the outcome of the author's own experience as a teacher in the elementary and high school grades and as a student in university art courses.

The study of each masterpiece is arranged to include, first, the story or interpretative introduction, the appreciative and technical study, and questions. Studies of pictures for the intermediate pupils include only the story and the questions. In every instance the story is the product of children's comments and suggestions in the classroom, reflecting their own experiences. In every case the teacher presenting the study in these grades should endeavor to develop the story with the active participation of the pupils. The questions are designed to aid in this part of the study. The stories included for the intermediate grades are suggestive only, and should not be used in such a way as to discourage the natural bent of the child to discover for himself the idea of the picture.

Under *Source of Subject* are given facts that may aid in appreciating the circumstances under which the composition was conceived.

A discussion of the essential principles of painting is included under *Setting, Arrangement, Light and Supreme Motive.* Here the material included is designed to give to the more advanced student an insight into some of the art principles which will help in laying the foundation for a broad appreciation.

Consistent with the general conception of the real test of a work of art, the supreme motive of the artist is studied at some length. Art is personal. A painter's conception is the expression of his innermost thought. Therefore, "It follows," wrote Ruskin, "that no vain or selfish person can possibly paint in the nobler sense of the word. Vanity and selfishness are troublous, eager, anxious, petulant;—painting can only be done in the calm of the mind."

Historical data are included for reasons that are obvious. The opinions of eminent art critics are given under *Comment*. The questions for study are purely suggestive and should be supplemented and adapted to the needs of the students. Facts of the artist's biography are made purposely meager. It is to be desired that the character of the painter be determined so far as possible from his conception itself.

The poetical and other quotations, it is believed, will prove especially worth while in the enjoyment of the sentiment expressed in the masterpieces.

The masterpieces which have been selected for study are those which are common to the majority of courses of study outlined for elementary and high schools.

To attempt to acknowledge all the sources from which the author has drawn in the preparation of this work would require greater space than this preface permits. Only a few of the most representative works are included in the reference list. Nevertheless, the author has endeavored to give in the text credit wherever it is due.

William C. Casey

INTRODUCTION

In order to sharpen the tongue or make facile the pen, to every youth is given, for study, examples of masters who have excelled in the use of spoken and written language. And to appreciate musical composition and harmony, we are trained to repeat the melodies of a Bach or Wagner. In like manner, to render practical, the powers of pictorial expression, the mind must be saturated with the excellencies of a Raphael and an Angelo, a Rembrandt and a Millet. Picture study is in a double sense cultural and educative.—Orr

TRUE WORKS OF ART

What is a truly great work of art? To appreciate the masterpiece, the standard of excellence must be determined. We drive into the open country. The landscape stretches away on every hand. Our impression of the fields and woods may be one thing; it is certain that the impression of the artist who takes his canvas and brush out to paint it, is quite another. Where we, lacking in the power of discernment and selection, come away without a definite, lasting impression in the broadest sense of the term, the artist, with his own keener susceptibilities and instinctive skill, selects, arranges and paints upon his canvas his own impression of that scene. If he is a great artist, but one dominating motive sways him. The motive that prompts the mother to direct her child prompts him to direct his painting. It may be a mournful note which he paints, or a gladsome, tuneful one. But the single, all-compelling idea is there, and his production will meet the test of true art only in so far as it stirs within us an appreciation for the beauty and mystery of God's manifold works.

Therefore we must establish the principle in the beginning that perfection in technique does not make the great artist. Yet that does not mean that a painter can produce a truly great picture without having mastered the technical skill of his art. Through a long life of study he acquires skill. But when his hand responds to the soul's inspiration, he casts aside the laws of men which bind him and creates the masterpiece.

Art can be defined as the process of developing a picture or object by means of incorporating the elements of texture, line, mass, shape and color in conjunction with the associated principles of harmony, repetition, contrast, balance and proportion for the purpose of communicating a message or to give visual pleasure.

In the Bible we read: "Whether therefore ye eat, or drink, or whatsoever ye do, do all to the glory of God." I Corinthians 10:31

This passage of Scripture challenges all people to approach each endeavor of life with the goal of pleasing God. The proper study of art, therefore, will inevitably point back to the author of all beauty—God.

The Creator Jesus Christ is obviously pleased with beauty, not merely utility. He is the original author of loveliness in all of its forms, and is clearly interested in creating things that are both functional and beautiful. God is the only artist who truly possesses an original genius—all other artists of the human variety can only reflect the genius and talent that God has given them.

Instructors should encourage their students to be thankful that the Lord created man with the ability to be creative and expressive. Since all human beings are created in God's image they should not be satisfied with a mediocre and drab existence. Art students should be trained to appreciate the beauty of good art and skilled in their efforts to constructively criticize those works of art that fail to measure up.

SELECTION OF PICTURES

After a consideration of these fundamentals in art, we may well ask, what pictures shall we place before the children? We who, perhaps, but once in a lifetime may enjoy the privilege of looking upon the original, have recourse only to the series of cheap but nonetheless excellent prints. The value of the study of such reproductions is sometimes questioned. We may answer:

> It is better to know art through reproduction than not to know it at all. It is only the best that can bear reproduction, and a good reproduction is a better preparation for the enjoyment of the original than a thousand pages of art criticism. To go from a photograph of the Sistine Madonna to the painting itself, is to have a dream come suddenly true with magnificent distinction. It is to see beauty in full sunlight after many twilight glimpses.—*Art Reproductions.*

UNDERLYING PRINCIPLES

Picture study based upon practical principles recognizes three periods in the development of the child. The beginner is interested in the picture only in so far as it reflects those things with which he meets in his everyday life. The little child reads into the picture his own experiences. He is primarily interested in the story. His world is one where color, music, life and action all abound. Scenes of homelife showing mother and father at work, brother and sister at play—these are the things in which he takes an active interest.

To the children of the intermediate grades come a livelier interest in and a fuller appreciation of the story which the painting tells. Pictures of occupations of men and women, boys and girls, in which activity is the keynote, hold the greatest appeal for them.

It is beginning with the grammar grades that with the appreciation of the story there comes to the adolescent an appreciation of how it is told. Elementary principles of composition will have an appeal. There comes in this period a broader interest in the artist's conception.

The method of approach in *Masterpieces In Art* recognizes these principles as the first essential in adapting the picture to the child. The picture itself is the basis of the study, no attempt being made to present a logical development of the history of painting.

The plan of study for the grammar and high school grades is designed to be more comprehensive. Here the interpretative introduction is aimed to create an atmosphere for the appreciation of the picture. In a number of instances the introductions have been wholly or in part suggested by comments and discussions in the classroom and reflect the attitude of average grammar grade pupils. They are not intended to hinder in any way the pupil's own interpretation of what he sees in the painting. They are intended to be suggestive, however, and are made as brief as is consistent with their purpose.

The questions are designed to assist both teacher and pupil in making a careful analysis of each study.

CONTENTS

ix

BIBLIOGRAPHY

GENERAL WORKS

Bates & Guild (Pub). *Masters in Art.*
Muther, Richard. *History of Modern Painting.*
Cook, Clarence. *Art and Artists of Our Time.*
John Ruskin. *Modern Painters.*
Woltmann and Woermann. *History of Painting.*
Mrs. Clement. *Handbook of Legendary Art.*
Mrs. Jameson. *Legends of the Madonna.*

SPECIAL APPRECIATION

Van Dyke, J. C. *How to Judge of a Picture.*
               Meaning of Pictures.
               Studies in Pictures.
               What Is Art?
Bradford, Armory H. *Messages of the Masters.*
Caffin, C. H. *How to Study Pictures.*
Harrison, Birge. *Landscape Painting.*
Hamerton, Philip Gilbert. *Imagination in Landscape Painting.*
Caffin, C. H. *A Child's Guide to Pictures.*
Emery, Mabel S. *How to Enjoy Pictures.*
Hind, Charles Lewis. *Adventures Among Pictures.*
Sturgis, Russel. *The Appreciation of Sculpture.*
               The Appreciation of Pictures.
Griggs, Edward Howard. *The Philosophy of Art.*
Greenshield. *Landscape Painting.*
L. C. Page & Co. (Pub). *Art Galleries of Europe and America.*
Powers, H. H. *Mornings with Masters of Art.*
Hamerton, P. G. *Thoughts About Art.*
La Farge, John. *Considerations on Painting.*

SCHOOLS

Caffin, C. H. *The Story of American Painting.*
Blashfield, Edwin H. *Mural Paintings in America.*
Cox, Kenyon. *Old Masters and New.*
De Forest, Julia B. *A Short History of Art.*
Radcliffe, A. G. *Schools and Masters of Painting.*
Symonds, John Addington. *Renaissance in Italy.*
Caffin, C. H. *American Masters of Sculpture.*
Whitcomb, Ida Prentice. *Young People's Story of Art.*
Stranahan, Mrs. C. H. *A History of French Painting.*
Van Dyke. *Old Dutch and Flemish Masters.*
Fromentin. *Old Masters of Belgium and Holland.*
Clement and Hutton. *Artists of the Nineteenth Century.*

WORLD PICTURES

The following list of paintings includes what a number of art critics agree upon as the twelve most celebrated pictures in the world. Those marked with a star are described in this manual.

Madonna di San Sisto (Sistine Madonna), Dresden Gallery— Raphael.

Assumption of the Virgin, Venice Academy—Titian.

The Transfiguration, Vatican Gallery, Rome—Raphael.

The Last Judgment, Sistine Chapel—Michelangelo.

Descent From the Cross, Antwerp Cathedral—Rubens.

The Night Watch, Amsterdam Gallery—Rembrandt.

Holy Night, Dresden Gallery—Correggio.

Immaculate Conception, Louvre, Paris—Murillo.

The Last Supper, Milan—Da Vinci.

Communion of St. Jerome, Vatican Gallery—Domenichino.

Descent From the Cross, Rome—Volterra.

Aurora, Rospigliosi Palace, Rome—Guido Reni.

THE FIRST STEP.—*Millet*

MASTERPIECES IN ART

THE FIRST STEP

Millet

Two little feet, so small that both may nestle
In one caressing hand,—
Two tender feet upon the untried border
Of life's mysterious land.
Love, for awhile, will make the path before them
All dainty, smooth, and fair,—
Will cut away the brambles, letting only
The roses blossom there.

—Anonymous

As Sensier remarks: Millet with nine children had abundant opportunity
to study them. This charming drawing was one of the collection of Millet's
pastels, formed by M. Gavet, which was unfortunately dispersed by auction
soon after the artist's death.—Low

THE PICTURE

Baby, baby, come to papa. See, his strong arms are outstretched to take you. Mamma will watch you. She will not
let you fall. Won't you try, dear little one?

Baby is learning to walk. He must try very hard. He
must take his first step. See, papa has thrown down his spade
to help him. Mamma, too, has stopped her work to lift him up.
How they must love their child.

Father toils all day for him. Here in the tiny garden he
is sowing the seed. He will care for the young plants. The
plants will make food. The food will make baby strong. See,

1

baby, papa rests on bended knee to take you. His great
strong arms will gently clasp you. Is he not a good father?
His work is very hard. The days are so long. His arms and
back grow very weary; but he never complains. He owns this
garden and a part of that great plain yonder. Is he not
proud to own all this? Then a glimpse of you, sweet baby,
lightens his work, and makes his arm stronger.

Baby, you must try. You must not take too much of father's
time. He still has much to do. Do you hear him coax you,
baby?

Yes, baby hears him. He crows with delight. He stretches
out his arms. He waves his hands. His eyes sparkle. He
jumps up and down with the joy of it all. The garden is so
pretty. The sunshine is so warm and bright. Baby longs to
toddle to papa. He longs to walk in the garden; but his little
legs are weak. He has never taken a step, and he is afraid to
leave mamma's arms.

Dear mamma, how tenderly she loves you, baby. She sings
to you in the morning. She rocks you to sleep at night. She
watches over you the livelong day. How she does want you to
try just now.

QUESTIONS

What are these people doing? In whom are they interested?
What is father saying? Why do we know? What is mother
saying? What is baby thinking? What is the expression on
his face? How does he show his feelings? Will he try to take
his first step? What makes you think so? Can you see the
expression on the man's face? Can we imagine what it might
be? Why did not the artist paint his face more plainly?
What does the artist wish us most to see? What has the
father been doing? The mother? How is the mother dressed?
The baby? The father? Are these people poor? Do they love
this little one? Where does your eye rest longest in the
picture? What sounds do you seem to hear? What actions do
you seem to see? What do you like best about this picture?
What do you think the artist is trying to say?

Only a baby small,
  Dropped from the skies,
Only a laughing face,
  Two sunny eyes;
Only two cherry lips,
  One chubby nose;
Only two little hands,
  Ten little toes.

Only a tender flower
  Sent us to rear;
Only a life to love
  While we are here;
Only a baby small
  Never at rest;
Small, but how dear to us,
  God knoweth best.

—Mathias Barr, *Only a Baby Small*

THE ARTIST

Millet, *Mĕ lā'*, **Jean François,** *Frän-swä'*, (1814—1875), was a French landscape painter, the most celebrated of the Barbizon group, which included Delacroix, Corot, Rousseau, Dupré and Troyon. He was born at Grouchy near Gréville, France. He was reared in a peasant home and as a youth worked in the fields with his father. He became a pupil of Dumouchel at Cherbourg in 1832, and in 1837 secured an annuity which enabled him to go to Paris, where he entered the studio of Paul Delaroche. He first exhibited in the Salon in 1840. City life was distasteful to him, and for a number of years he had a continuous struggle with the critics.

In 1849 Millet went to Barbizon and resumed the peasant life of his youth. Here he remained and labored until his death in 1875. He painted about eighty pictures. He won honors at the World Exposition of 1867; and is now represented in the Louvre Gallery, Paris; the Metropolitan Museum of Art, New York; the Museum of Fine Arts, Boston; the Art Institute, Chicago; and other national galleries and private collections.

Millet's life itself explains his art. Never have heart and hand, a man and his work, tallied with each other as they did in him.—Muther

THE GLEANERS

Millet

There's a merry laughter in the field
And the harmless jest and frolic rout
And the last harvest van goes by
With its rustling load so pleasantly
To the glad and clamorous harvest shout.

THE PICTURE

What a busy scene! How familiar it is, too. We need not be told that it is the glorious harvest time in this great field. The acres and acres of brown stubble shorn of its golden harvest speak plainly of this most welcome season of the year.

Could a more delightful picture be imagined? Far to the right in the background the little cluster of homes with its fringe of trees basks in the sunshine. At the left, two mountain-like stacks of grain speak of the richness of the yield.

How busily the men are working. Some are binding the wheat into sheaves while others are pitching it upon the wagon. Still others are piling sheaf upon sheaf until the stacks tower high above them. Far to the right an overseer mounted upon a horse is watching the labor.

But what is the meaning of this strange group in the foreground? Surely we have never seen in our fields such labor as this. What can these three women be doing?

A long, long time ago when God had brought His chosen people into a very rich country, he had thus charged them:

And when ye reap the harvest of your land, thou shalt not wholly reap the corners of thy field, neither shalt thou gather the gleanings of thy harvest . . . thou shalt leave them for the poor and stranger.— Leviticus xix:9, 10.

4

THE GLEANERS.—*Millet*

Today these three poor but thrifty women have come to this field to glean. How eagerly they are searching among the stubble for the few stray stalks. Not an instant do they pause. Together they move as their hands clutch the blades, one by one.

What strong figures. How firmly they seem to stand upon the ground. Nearest us, the eldest woman is somewhat alone in her efforts to gather the grain. Unlike her two companions, she cannot endure long at a time the painful stooping position. She is now bending awkwardly, the task is so painful to her.

How easily the woman in the center of the group moves. Her back, so strong and broad, speaks of the heavy burdens it has borne. Her right arm is reaching forward as the rough, toilworn hand grasps each bit of grain. How solidly her foot with its broad wooden shoe rests upon the ground. At her side the youngest of the three moves more gracefully and more easily. She wears no apron, satisfied to carry her gleanings in her left hand, which rests palm upward upon her back. The hand is shapely because its owner is young.

How lifelike is the action of these figures. We seem to see their movement completed. Carefully they thread their way through the sharp stubble. So boldly are their bent forms drawn, that we might easily walk in and out among them.

How coarsely but neatly they are dressed. Their poverty may show in their clothing, but they are tidy. The two older women have folded their aprons to hold the grain, while all three wear kerchiefs over their heads looped in front to shade their eyes.

The morning is well advanced. The harvest sun is high and throws its heat over the field. The harvesters in the distance are merrily hauling their last load, but the gleaners are concerned only with their own task.

In the distance are the homes where their influence is felt in the tidy rooms and the clean homeyards, and where the manifold tasks of shearing, carding, spinning, weaving and sewing all fall to them.

They work with perfect contentment. It makes no difference to them that the harvest of another is gathered up in sheaves while they must gather the stray stalks one by one. They do not envy the great stacks so near, beside which their own slim bundles seem as nothing. What lives in all the world are more heroic!

> He that is down needs fear no fall,
> He that is low, no pride;
> He that is humble ever shall
> Have God to be his guide.
>
> I am content with what I have,
> Little be it or much:
> And, Lord, contentment still I crave,
> Because Thou savest such.
>
> Fullness to such a burden is
> That go on pilgrimage:
> Here little, and hereafter bliss,
> Is best from age to age.

—John Bunyan

PLAN FOR STUDY

1. **Source of Subject.** *The Gleaners* represents another phase of the never-ending round of labor upon Barbizon plain. We are told that the model used in this subject was Mere Marier, a peasant woman in the village. We must not, however, understand from this that the artist used models other than for the merest suggestions. He chose rather to rely upon impressions which had been imprinted upon his mind as he watched the actual labor in the fields.

2. **Setting.** In the background the great stacks, the heavily loaded wagon, and the bulging sheaves are suggestive of a bountiful harvest, in contrast with the painfully slim bundles gathered by the gleaners in the foreground. This is a typical harvest scene under an August sky. The plain soil-stained dresses of the women are in perfect keeping with their work. There is an impression of heat, even sultriness, in the scene, and of its effect in making doubly hard and wearisome the toil of the women. Their gleanings, straw by straw, seem pathetically poor and inadequate.

The great expanse of plain and its limitless character is a feature much emphasized in all Millet's pictures. It is as if he would suggest in the monotony of such a setting the unchanging tenor of the toiler's life. There is a suggestion of the village in the right foreground.

3. **Arrangement.** This is a characteristic Millet composition—industry framed in a limitless landscape. Here, however, are more details than are usually found in his subjects. The women are arranged in the foreground, while in the background, somewhat indistinctly portrayed, is the real harvesting—overseer, men, sheaves, shocks, wagon and stacks. To the right are seen the roofs and trees of the village. The most characteristic quality is the sense of motion in the three women. Observe how the lines of the arms and forms contrasted with the vertical lines of the sides of the picture help to give this effect; also that the predominant lines of the plain are horizontal and are repeated in the horizon line and the sky, giving a note of repose. The monotony of the horizontal is broken by the curved stacks, the slanting lines of the roofs, and the perpendicular lines in the form of the overseer.

How skilfully is arranged the balance—the stacks with the roofs, the wagon with the overseer on horseback, the two left figures of the gleaners with the one on the right. Note the effect of perspective—the varying degrees of distinctness in the objects of the different planes. Study the different attitudes in the forms of the women—the buoyancy of youth in the girl to the left, the stolid, experienced air of the middle-aged woman in the center, both contrasted with the painfully rheumatic figure of the oldest woman on the right. It was a fine touch which pictured these women in the three ages of life. Observe the rendering of their dresses. How severely plain they are, without pleat or fold to detract from the action of the figures.

4. **Center of Interest.** It would be quite natural to infer that the three gleaners from their size, their prominent position in the foreground, the lighting and the title form the center of interest. True, they are the chief figures, but, observes one, if we note carefully the trend of the leading lines we find that they converge upon the real harvesting in the central background.

5. **Supreme Motive.** Again we have the supreme idea of Millet, the courage, patience and industry of the toilers. The pathos of their scanty reward in the shadow of superabundance, the fate which has reduced them to such straits, and their humility, patience and faithfulness in the face of it all make a profound impression. There is a distinct appeal made to our better selves. We are inclined to question a social order where such inequality is possible, and critics have accused Millet of inspiring just this sort of social unrest.

This painting called forth a storm of criticism from those who professed to know of no such drudgery among the peasant toilers. But this was far from Millet's purpose. He saw the beauty in their faithful performance of duty. He said, "It is impossible simply to depict the ideas that come into one's mind at the sight of the man who eats bread in the sweat of his face!" He did not strive for pretty effects; he sought to paint the truth. These women do not ask for our sympathy, they do not complain, they do not falter. That the honest sweat trickles down their worn faces, that they are weary, that their backs ache, that their hands are knotted and hardened with toil, they do not deny. But the nobility of it all as they uncomplainingly accept their lot, and with fortitude and diligence labor through the weary years in that sphere in which fate has decreed they should work is the truth Millet sought to express in this subject.

Some, however, are inclined to differ with Millet in his conception of the peasant. Their point of view is summed up in this excerpt from Mrs. Ellen Russel Emerson's *Nature and Human Nature:*

This peasant artist presents a picture of unintelligent toil, and the possibilities which lie at every point of human life where toil may be subordinated into automatic activity—the mind set free to blazon a path to higher matters—are unwittingly represented in the sweep of his brush in aerial perspective, as also the cradling environment of nature, calm, permanent, and unviolable: that temple of God and his hosts whose entrance is given him who seeks it. . . . The toiler without aspiration, the gleaner without ideals . . . are the themes of pessimism, but happily they do not prevail, for the sun shines and God is good.

6. Light and Shade. We judge from the short shadows that the sun is well up. This picture is typical of that rendering of light and air in which Millet always excelled. The sun is a unifying feature. The dark of the figures, brought up against the ground, gives them bulk and shape. Note the impression we get of their feet firmly pressing upon the ground. Observe the high light on the harvesters. What does this signify as to the center of interest in the scene? There is a feeling of space between the three women.

7. Color. The colors are subdued. Red is the prevailing tone in the dress of the women, and this with the other colors, brown and green, is modified with the earth stains and bits of straw which cling to their garments.

8. History. *The Gleaners* was exhibited in the Salon of 1867. Millet through Jules Dupré sold it to M. Binder of the Isle-Adam for $400. In 1889 it was sold to Madame Veuve Pommery of Rheims for $60,000, on condition that it should eventually be presented to the Louvre. This was done and it now hangs in that celebrated gallery.

COMMENT

No artist has ever surpassed him in the power of rendering air,—the extent of the plain which only ends with the horizon, the depth of the sky which human eye cannot penetrate.

The Gleaners from every point of view is among the most important and most complete of Millet's works.—Mantz

The one great object he placed before him was truth. He painted Nature as he found her.—Staley

Millet did not draw his figures from the model. He had so saturated his mind with the attitude and gestures of the people at work, whether in action or in repose, that he could reproduce them at will.—Cook

The simple dignity of his figures is universally known, and they are usually engaged in the most humble occupations. He did not flatter his peasant models on the score of physical beauty: but when he observed some unconscious nobility in the carriage or gesture, he never failed to make the most of it.—Hamerton

QUESTIONS

What are these women doing? What does it mean to glean? What is being done in the field behind them? What time of year is it? What time of day? How do you know? In what respects are the women in the foreground different? Are they weary? Are they contented? Which seems most tired? Why, do you suppose? Which seems to be the youngest? Why do you think so? Have they gathered much grain? How do they gather it? How are the men gathering it? How are the women dressed? Where do they live? What other tasks are they called upon to do? Where is the most interesting part of the picture? Why? Where is the center of interest? What do you think the artist tried to say in this picture? Has he said it plainly? Do you think he admired these workers? For what qualities do you think he admired them?

What in the setting suggests the nature of the industry? Where did the custom of gleaning originate? What are the dominant lines in this composition? What general impression do they give? What is the center of interest? How emphasized? What does the lighting accomplish? Just what is the appeal which the picture makes to you? In what respects is it similar to others of the artist's pictures?

FEEDING HER BIRDS

Millet

My heart is like a fountain true
That flows and flows with love to you.
As chirps the lark unto the tree
So chirps my pretty babe to me.
And it's O! sweet, sweet! and a lullaby.

The Queen has sceptre, crown and ball,
You are my sceptre, crown and all.
For all her robes of royal silk,
More fair your skin, and white as milk.
And it's O! sweet, sweet! and a lullaby.

—Anonymous

What the leaves are to the forest,
With light and air for food,
Ere their sweet and tender juices
Have been hardened into wood,—

That to the world are children;
Through them it feels the glow
Of a brighter and sunnier climate
Than reaches the trunks below.

—Longfellow, *Children*

THE PICTURE

"Come, little ones, here is a surprise for you." Three
little children at play in the sunny dooryard hear mamma's
voice. Three pairs of wondering eyes see mamma with a
steaming bowl in her hands standing in the doorway. Little
brother drops his cart, one little sister her basket of shells and
the other catches up her doll. All run to mamma.

See, here they are all snuggled together on the sunny door-
step. Their mother, seated on a stool, is about to give them

12

FEEDING HER BIRDS.—*Millet*

some food. She holds the bowl in her lap, and with the wooden spoon she will give each a generous share. How eagerly each awaits his turn. Mamma, busy, loving, kindly mamma that she is, has put aside her many cares for a moment to give the children a surprise. How she loves them. How carefully she holds the spoon. The budding rose vines clambering over the walls smile down upon the little group. A few hens are clucking hungrily for the stray bits that may fall. What serious faces the children have. How quiet they are just now. Can you not see the reason? Mamma is holding a spoonful out to baby brother. Of course he must have the first taste. Be careful, Jean, or the food will spill. The mouths of all are wide open; one sister caresses her brother, the other fondles her doll. We cannot see the mother's face plainly, but we know it must have a kind, loving expression. Papa works nearby. His strong arm must turn the soil and plant the seed, for these little ones depend upon him. The sight of them through the gate makes his heart glad, his arm stronger and his work lighter. The artist who painted the picture said:

"When I paint a mother, I try to render her beautiful, by the tender look she gives her child."

PLAN FOR STUDY

1. **Source of Subject.** The dooryard sketches, *Feeding Her Birds, Feeding the Hens, First Steps,* and others, are impressions of the artist's own home life in Barbizon. Millet's home was his special delight. Within his little enclosure, shut off from public gaze, the daily tasks were enlivened by the play and prattle of children. Here was the vine-covered cottage with its walls of stone and roof of tile; here was the garden with its trees, shrubs and vegetables, the whole beautified by the flowers which blossomed in profusion, and here Millet romped and played with his children, whom he dearly loved.

2. **Setting.** The scene represents a typical dooryard in Barbizon. Note the homely details in the setting and what each

contributes to the general impression. The dress of the mother and the frocks and sabots of the children are coarse and ugly, but neat and whole, in a word, respectable. The rude little cart and basket on the ground are products of the father's handiwork; the hens in the gateway suggest an important adjunct to the cottage. The walls are old, and the yard itself is without ornament, save nature's own contribution in the form of vines over door and window. All is suggestive of a very humble, poor, limited homelife, yet a respectable and thoroughly satisfactory one to this happy little family.

3. **Arrangement.** We have the painter's own statement that in this picture he wished to suggest a little brood of nestlings, the mother feeding them, and the father nearby working for them all. Note how well he has succeeded in giving that impression. The chief figures, the mother and children, are arranged in the foreground. The little ones are snuggled closely together in the doorway, suggesting a crowded nest, the mother bends over them, tilting the stool on which she is seated, the better to bring her nearer, in an attitude not unlike that of the mother bird. The bowl is held in her left hand, her right reaches out the spoonful of food to the youngest or "baby bird."

The position of the woman on a level with the children serves to bring us also to the same level, where we look into the fresh little faces, even as she does. What serious and decorus little people they are. The girls, themselves not much older, with charming unselfishness and sisterly affection, wait patiently until the baby brother is served. Little white caps catch and hold back from their faces the stray ringlets, while the brother is favored with a highly decorated round hat, button and all. In the glimpse of the great out-of-doors through the gate, we see the father toiling in the garden, and this adds a pleasing note of parental love and sacrifice.

Observe the principle of perspective as applied here in representing the father's figure and the details of the garden. Note the effect of the spoon in the mother's hand, of the fowls in the gateway and of the glimpse of the man in holding our interest in the lower level of the picture. This serves to counteract the suggestion of aspiration and solemnity which might otherwise be emphasized, because of the predominating vertical lines of door, vine and window.

4. **Center of Interest.** The tip of the spoon is emphasized above all other objects. This is accomplished by the high light and by the direction of the interest of the chief figures. The mother watches it closely to bring it to the open mouth of the youngest without spilling the contents. Every faculty of the child is bent on receiving it; the little sisters wait its approach just as anxiously; even the interest of the nearest fowl is centered upon it. Draw a vertical and a horizontal line across the composition so that they will intersect at the tip of the spoon and study the spacing thus effected. Is it similar to others of the artist's compositions?

5. **Supreme Motive.** The alert child who studies this picture will divine the idea of the painter quite as well as the experienced critic. Millet himself said of the picture, which was one of his favorites, "In the *Woman Feeding Her Birds* I want to suggest a nest of birds with their mother giving them food, the man in the distance working for them all." The painter realized his power in enlisting the interest and sympathy when he gave us this simple scene. A warm heart is always moved by its appeal.

6. **Light and Shade.** Observe the important contribution the lighting makes to the general charm of the subject. It is a warm sunlight which streams full upon the scene and gathers every detail into one harmonious whole. We see the characteristic treatment of the chief figures in relieving the dark figure of the mother against the light gray of the wall. The shadows show that the light comes from the right. It touches the cap of the woman and lights up the faces of the children. See how the little sabots are rounded out against the light gray of the ground. Note the suggestion of airy space between the form of the mother and the wall; also how the dark in the figures below is repeated in the foliage overhead, and how these dark tones merge gradually into the lighter gray ones. This shading effect is one of the points of beauty in the composition.

7. **History.** This picture was painted in 1860, and in the following year was exhibited in the Salon. It passed into the Museum of Lille in 1871, where it now hangs.

QUESTIONS

What do you see first in the picture? What is the woman doing? At what are the children looking? What have they been doing? How do you know? What is the expression on their faces? Are they happy? Why? Is the expression the same on every face? How is the mother feeding them? How is she dressed? Does she look like mothers you know? How are the children dressed? What are these queer things they wear upon their feet? Where do these children live? Are they poor? How do you know? Who is the man just outside the gate? What is he doing? For whom is he working? What else do you see in the picture? Have you ever seen homes like this one? Where? How do we know this mother loves her children? Whom is she feeding first? Is this quite fair? Where does the light come from? Where does your eye rest the longest? Where is the center of interest? How do you know? Why do you suppose the artist named this picture *Feeding Her Birds?* What do you think he is trying to tell us in it? Does he tell it plainly? Do you think the artist loved children? Why do you think so? Do you think he loved his home? Why do you think so?

> Blessings, blessings on the beds
> Whose white pillows softly bear,
> Rows of little shining heads
> That have never known a care.
>
> Pity for the heart that bleeds
> In the homestead desolate
> Where no little troubling needs
> Make the weary working wait.
>
> Safely, safely to the fold
> Bring them wheresoe'er they be,
> Thou, who saidst of them, of old,
> "Suffer them to come to me."

> —Alice Cary

THE SOWER

Millet

Brethren, the sower's task is done.
The seed is in its winter bed.
Now let the dark-brown mould be spread,
To hide it from the sun,
And leave it to the kindly care
Of the still earth and brooding air,
The tempest now may smite the sleet,
All night on the drowned furrow beat,
And winds that, from the cloudy hold,
Of winter breathe the bitter cold,
Stiffen to stone the mellow mould,
Yet safe shall lie the wheat;
Till, out of heaven's unmeasured blue,
Shall walk again the genial year,
To wake with warmth and nurse with dew
The germs we lay to slumber here.

—Bryant, *Song of the Sower*

THE PICTURE

What a simple scene. Yet what charm it has for us. The great field rising to an upland forms a background against which the figure of the Sower stands out strongly. In the distance on the other side of the slope the last rays of the sun light up a group of oxen drawing a plow. Such a time as this when

The fresh dark acres furrowed lie,
And ask the Sower's hand

always delighted Millet. "The most delightful thing I know," he once said, "is the peace, the silence that one enjoys on the tilled lands. It is here that I find the true humanity, the great poetry."

18

THE SOWER.—*Millet*

What a lordly figure. What strength is revealed in the gesture of arm and swing of body. Against the darkening sky and shadowy field the man stands out so strong and lifelike that it seems as if we might see his swinging stride carry him down the slope and out of sight.

There is all the fire of youth in the swing of the great body which even the coarse peasant's garb does not conceal. A faded weather-worn hat is pulled well down over the head, while clumsy wooden shoes protect the feet.

Early in the freshness and beauty of a bright spring morning the Sower strapped the sack of seed to his back and went forth to sow. All day long he has trudged steadily to and fro. In his left hand he grasps the flap of the pouch which holds the grain; with his right, he scatters the precious seed in great waves evenly over the ground.

True to the rule in olden lore which bids the sower cast the seed crosswise into the air would he hope for an abundant harvest, this sower throws the grain. So lifelike is his action that we seem to see the right arm swing upward and across as it completes the movement. With the poet we feel like calling to him,

> Fling wide the golden shower; we trust
> The strength of armies to the dust.
> Nay, strew with free and joyous sweep,
> The seed upon the expecting soil;
> For hence the plenteous year shall heap
> The garners of the men who toil.

> —Bryant

He knows the importance of careful sowing. His loved ones at home depend upon the outcome of his work. Without a rich harvest they must suffer. Then, too, does not the whole world look for its bread to the strong right arm that sows the seed?

Well this man knows the price which earth asks for all she gives. From experience he can measure the labor which cleared this field of last year's stubble and turned it into furrows. Now, as he scatters the seed, he realizes full well that before the crop shall be gathered the scorching sun of the harvest must be braved. But he is not discouraged. Experience has taught him that nature rewards generously from out her own vast store such faithful labor.

How pathetic this man's life seems to us. From earliest boyhood he has labored upon this very plain. The future holds no better promise for him than this day's toil. Little wonder that the hopelessness of such a life appealed to the artist. Yet we may be sure that he does not desire our sympathy. His calling may be humble, but he is proud of it. His peasant garb may be coarse, but it is nevertheless as becoming to him as is the flashing uniform to the general. There is perfect contentment in his bearing; a satisfaction in knowing work well done.

> Give me, ye God , the product of one field,
> That so I neither may be rich nor poor;
> And having just enough, not covet more.

—Dryden

> Give fools their gold and knaves their power;
> Let fortune's buffer rise and fall;
> Who sows a field or trains a flower,
> Or plants a tree is more than all.

> For he who blesses most is blest;
> And God and man shall own his worth
> Who toils to leave as his bequest
> An added beauty to the earth.

—Whittier

PLAN FOR STUDY

1. **Source of Subject.** A sower at work in the fields of Barbizon is the artist's subject. Barbizon is a farming community in central France, famous at the present time for the great painters who lived and worked there, and also for its proximity to the most beautiful part of the forest of Fontainebleau, the largest forest reserve in France.

2. **Setting.** The shadowy field and sky speak of the close of day. A note of repose dominates, and in such a setting the action of the stalwart figure is more strongly emphasized. The newly broken ground is suggestive of that "cry of the

soil'' which Millet was so anxious to express in his pictures. The flocks of birds following in the Sower's wake just over the hilltop suggest the seedtime. Observe also the soil-stained garb of the man and how it is in accord with the prevailing note—labor. The pouch securely held and the shower of seed suggest the nature of the work; the plowman in the background indicates the preparation of the soil for the sowing.

3. **Arrangement.** The distinguishing feature of all Millet's pictures is the simplicity of his compositions. They rarely deal with more than one or two figures, and in nearly every case the landscape is bare of any details which might detract from the all-absorbing industry pictured in the foreground. This picture is one of his simplest compositions—remarkable for its suggestive qualities.

Suggestion in literature, observes one, is oftentimes the most effective means of impressing the greatest truths. Let us try to understand the significance of this statement in our subject for study. In the arrangement we see at once that the predominating feature is the man himself. By his position and size he is made the chief object. However, it is the action of the figure that engages the interest. Note that this action is effected by the variety of lines. There is first the slanting line of the slope, repeated in the lines of the furrows. The slanting lines of arms and legs in contrast with the vertical lines of the sides of the picture also emphasize the idea of motion. Observe the effect of the plowman in the right background in breaking the monotony of the horizontal lines. See how completely he and his oxen are subordinated, marking that plane in the composition in which objects are indistinct through the atmosphere.

4. **Center of Interest.** As noted in the arrangement, the Sower is the center of interest. Note the power of suggestion in the sturdy figure. As is true of all his peasants, the artist here has given us a type. The day is done, darkness is lowering, the Sower's toil must soon cease. His figure is very real and strong and lifelike in the gathering gloom. Against the sky his head and shoulders are sharply featured, while the rest of his body is comparatively shrouded against the dark of the

hill. Note the effect of this in serving to bind the man closely to the soil. His feet press firmly against it, his body seems a part of it, making an effective union of the man and his work. A long stride has brought the right foot forward, and the body rests almost equally upon both feet. Observe the length of the stride and what it signifies as to the swiftness of the man's movement. Note the indistinctness of his features and the simplicity of the lines of his figure. The artist by this intimates that he is not concerned with an individual peasant, but rather that he seeks to give us a peasant type.

5. **Supreme Motive.** It has been often said that art deals with that which is beautiful in nature. Wherein lies the beauty of this subject? It is the aim of every true artist to discover some hidden beauty in the world about him and to reveal it in his paintings. Millet, the peasant painter in the fields of Barbizon, saw a never ending round of labor. Because he himself had been one of the laborers he knew all phases of the peasant's life. He knew the tiny sphere in which he moved; the hopelessness of his daily round; and his courage, honesty and patience in performing his task.

To Millet the humble toiler was a heroic type. His peasants certainly have little of beauty about them, and this subject is devoid of beauty unless we are able to appreciate the artist's idea. Millet said:

Beauty does not lie in the face, it lies in the harmony between the man and his toil. . . . I wish that the beings I represent should have the air of dedication to their positions, and that they should not suggest any other.

Is not all this represented in this sturdy figure? Does not this man feel the responsibility of his task? The bigness of his movement as though he would encompass the field? The great world that looks to the strong right arm for bread will not be disappointed. His is the type that will not falter in the performance of duty, however humble and wearisome it may be. The largeness of his task does not overwhelm, it inspires him. Herein lies the nobility of the toiler, and such we believe to be the conception of the peasant-painter.

6. Light and Shade. The setting sun touches the sky with the glorious evening splendor Millet knew so well how to represent. Twilight is coming on. The plowed land, bathed in shadow, occupies nearly two-thirds of the canvas. Observe the effect of the slope brought up against the glow of the sky —how the spacing of the dark and light of the background is just right to give a note of restfulness to the scene. What would be the effect if the sky occupied a greater space? Note how the strongest dark of the figure is brought up against the light of the sky, giving it bulk and shape, and how the lighter portion of the figure against the black produces the same effect.

7. History. *The Sower* was painted in 1850 for the Salon of that year. The artist had several times before sketched this subject, but this sketch is the most satisfactory. This picture and *The Gleaners* were at first harshly criticized, many claiming that in this the artist purposely showed the dark side of the peasant's life. The picture passed finally into the Vanderbilt Collection, New York City, and now hangs in the Vanderbilt Loan Collection at the Metropolitan Museum of Art. Size of canvas: Seventeen and seven-eighths inches high, two feet eight and five-eighths inches wide.

COMMENT

His *Sower*, his *Man with the Hoe*, his *Shepherdess* are heroic types of their order, and sum up the story of whole generations of toilers. They represent all that is noblest and most pathetic in that peasant-life Millet knew so well, all the deeper meanings and larger truths which lie hidden beneath the surface.—Cartwright

While patiently studying the action of his reapers, Millet produced a figure which had long occupied his thoughts. We know what a serious affair the sowing is to an agricultural people. Plowing, manuring and harrowing are done with comparative indifference, at any rate without heroic passion; but when a man puts on the white grain-bag, rolls it around his left arm, fills it with seed, the hope of the coming year, that man exercises a sort of sacred ministry. He says nothing, looks straight before him, measures the furrow, and, with a movement cadenced like the rhythm of a mysterious song, throws the grain which falls to the earth and will soon be covered by the harrow. The rhythmic walk of the sower and his action are superb. The importance of the deed is real, and he feels his responsibility. If he is a good laborer he will know how much seed to throw with every fling of his hand, adjusting the amount sown to the nature of the soil. I have seen sowers who, before they put foot upon the field, would toss a handful of grain into the air in the sign of a cross; then stepping upon the field, they would pronounce, in a low voice, some indistinct words which sounded like a prayer.—Sensier, *Life of Millet*

QUESTIONS

What is the predominating note in the setting? What is the occupation of the single figure? What points to this? Is his movement swift or slow? How did you get your impression? Does the Sower show a spirit of "dedication" to his task? If so, in what way? What are the predominating lines? Their effect? Explain how the figure is well-balanced. What in the artist's life would especially fit him to picture this toiler sympathetically? What is the supreme motive in this subject? Does this picture record the artist's own impression of the scene, or is it merely a truthful copy of what he saw? What is meant when we speak of the Sower as a type, not as an individual? Wherein does the artist represent this subject as a type? How are we impressed with the unity in the sower and his task? What are some of the qualities of his type? Do you find any of those qualities revealed in this figure? Just what in his calling seems heroic? Do you think the artist has selected the best time of the day for the setting? Why? Do you think the landscape is quite satisfactory? Why? Why are the plowman, his plow and team so indistinct? Why are they shown in the picture at all? In what respects is this subject similar to others by the same artist?

THE SHEEP FOLD

Jacque

How sweet is the shepherd's sweet lot!
From the morn to the evening he strays;
He shall follow his sheep all the day,
And his tongue shall be filled with praise.
For he hears the lamb's innocent call,
And he hears the ewe's tender reply;
He is watchful, while they are in peace,
For they know when their Shepherd is nigh.

—Wm. Blake, *The Shepherd*

THE PICTURE

How contented these sheep seem. Some are eating the hay which has been tossed down to them. Others are drinking from the tub of clear water. A few hens have strayed in from the frosty air without. They are clucking contentedly as they peck at the bits of grain. Their sharp eyes search out every morsel as they scratch. One has crept near the feeding rack. Others are content to rest in the clean straw on the floor.

Is it not all very interesting and charming? How these peaceful sheep interest us. Their thick coats of wool are very real in the bright light which beams upon them. How secure they seem. They know they are safe from harm. The good shepherd who cares for them has never failed them. In the springtime he leads them to fresh pastures and pure water. He keeps them from poisonous weeds and protects them from wild animals. In the winter season, when bitter winds sweep the meadow, he provides for them this warm shelter.

Do these sheep miss the sunny meadow with its green grass? Indeed they do. But it is now covered with snow. The short winter days must be spent within these walls, but the fold is

26

THE SHEEP FOLD.—*Jacque*

very comfortable. Clean straw is strewn upon the floor, and they have an abundance to eat and drink.

What do these sheep give the shepherd in return for all this? They obey his every call. They give him their warm wool, which is carded, spun and woven, and made into warm clothing for the shepherd and his family. He sells some of the wool and with the money buys food and other necessities for his family.

Feed on, gentle sheep. The sun is slowly slipping away in the west. The shadows will soon creep into your fold. The sand man will make your eyes heavy, and you will lie down and sleep. But never fear; the fold is secure; its walls are strong; its door is barred; and no harm can come to you.

This picture was painted in 1870. It is known as *The Sheep Fold* and also as *Feeding the Sheep*.

PLAN FOR STUDY

For the study of this picture use the plan given for the study of *Sheep. Autumn* by Mauve.

QUESTIONS

What is this picture about? What has brought the flock to the fold? What is their general expression? Who cares for the sheep? Have you ever seen him care for them in the pasture? What does the shepherd do for them? What do they do for him in return? What are the most natural things about this scene? What season of the year is represented? Why do you suppose the artist has represented the hens in this scene? Are all the sheep doing the same thing? Point out their different positions. What is the expression of this one drinking from the tub? Of those looking at us? Do the sheep act naturally? How is their food stored for them in the fold? From what direction does the light come? Does it add anything to the picture? What? What time of day is it? How does the artist show this? Where is the brightest light? The darkest spot? Where did your eye rest first in the scene?

Where is the center of interest? What thoughts does this picture suggest to you? What one thing does it seem to say? What thoughts probably helped the artist in representing these sheep? What are the most pleasing things about the picture? What one thing do you like best about it? Does it suggest a story to you? What?

THE ARTIST

Jacque, *Zhawk,* **Charles Émile** (1813—1890), a French painter and engraver, was born in Paris. He is chiefly known for his paintings of sheep. He made no important exhibits until after 1846. In 1867 he was given the Decoration of the Legion of Honor, and he won a first-class medal at the Paris Exposition in 1889.

His canvases are always small, but his workmanship is broad and masculine.

SHEEP. AUTUMN

Mauve

All service ranks the same with God—
With God, whose puppets, best and worst,
Are we; there is no last nor first.

—Robert Browning

He toils at e'en, he toils at morn,
His work is never through;
A coming life o' weary toil
Is ever in his view.
But on he trudges, keeping aye
A stout heart to the brae,
And proud to be an honest man
Until his dying day.

—Robert Nicoll

THE PICTURE

In this painting of sheep in a landscape touched with the
red and gold of autumn, there is a wealth of tenderness and
a tinge of sadness. The sturdy old man accompanied by his
dog is walking slowly homeward with his flock as the sunset
rays touch the fields with a last lingering glow. In the early
morning he led his flock to the pasture. There they nibbled
the grass while the old shepherd,

Singing all day long, his flocks he learns to keep;
Himself as innocent as are his simple sheep.

—Giles Fletcher

Perhaps he slept away many of the long, tedious hours,
perfectly content to trust the sheep to the care of the watch-
dog trotting alone at his side. The little animal has cared for
them well, and at the close of day, barking loudly as he runs
here and there, has started the stragglers in a compact mass on

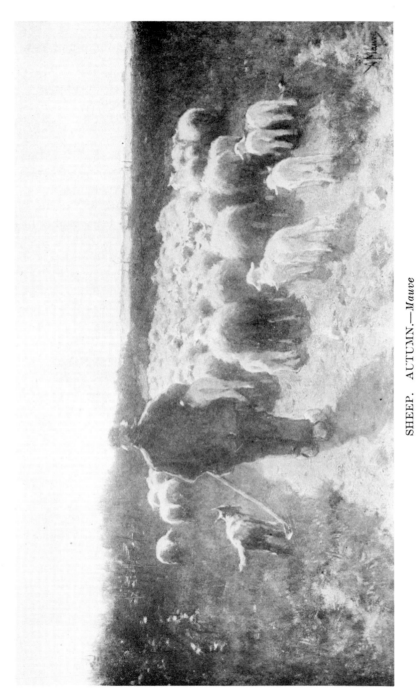

SHEEP. AUTUMN.—*Mauve*

their homeward journey. His hardest task is done and now
he follows behind them,

> Patient, full of importance, and grand in the pride of his instinct,
> Walking from side to side with a lordly air, and superbly
> Waving his bushy tail, and urging forward the stragglers.
>
> —Longfellow

Near the head of the column a few unruly ones have become
separated from the rest in their search for one more morsel
of grass. They will not be allowed to stray far, however, for
the dog's keen eyes are upon them. A member of the flock,
perhaps a wounded one, is being carried in the shepherd's
arms.

In the distance a glimpse of the sea conveys the idea of the
boundless character of the plain. Beyond the water is a faint
suggestion of other lands, cities and homes. Above, stretches
the expanse of sky, somewhat cloudy in the twilight of an
autumn day.

A thoughtful silence rests upon the landscape. The thickets
which border the path in the distance speak of the seared and
brown leaves of autumn. Even the grass is losing much of its
freshness and verdure. The whole landscape seems pervaded
by the thought expressed by Whittier:

> Gone hath the Spring, with all its flowers,
>   And gone the Summer's pomp and show,
> And Autumn, in his leafless bowers,
>   Is waiting for the Winter's snow.

While nature alone might suggest the autumn, the artist
has given us in the person of the old herdsman another suggestion of the same season. As a youth, as a young man, and
now as the old shepherd in this picture, he has passed the
lonesome hours of a lifetime upon the plain. His long life of
service inspired the artist to paint him in the fields when the
last traces of the summer blend into the dreary winter season.
As the day is nearing its close, so is he approaching the sunset
of his life. The autumn comes as a sign that the growing
season is ended. With all the gentleness and sympathy of the
painter we are made to feel that in like manner the autumn

time in the patient figure has been reached. We see a deeper meaning in the sunset when we study the form of the old man. The slanting rays of the sun glide along the backs of the sheep and flood the path with brightness. The silvery gray of the sky and of the distant water, the brown and green of the foliage, all bathed in the mellow light of the sun's last rays, blend into a perfect harmony of color. The soft, golden glow envelopes everything and the very spirit of autumn and the close of day permeates the picture.

PLAN FOR STUDY

1. **Source of Subject.** Like Millet of France, Mauve was more impressed with the life of the shepherd than that of any other toiler. The loneliness of such a life, with its pathetic side, was often represented by him. To the painters of Holland, and especially to Mauve, we owe something of our best impressions of the poetic side of a shepherd's life.

> Where the quiet-colored end of evening smiles,
> Miles on miles,
> On the solitary pastures where our sheep,
> Half asleep,
> Tinkle homeward thro' the twilight, stray or stop
> As they crop.
> —Robert Browning

2. **Setting.** A more beautiful setting for the old man and his sheep could scarcely be imagined. This is due not alone to the landscape, but to the fitness of such a figure trudging along at the close of day in the autumn season. Then, too, sheep always add to the charm and interest of a landscape. Typical of gentleness, trust and repose, they are the chief contribution to the general impression conveyed by this setting. All nature suggests the autumn, and the bowed form of the old shepherd gives yet another suggestion of the same season.

3. **Arrangement.** The artist has employed a very common method of arrangement. The principal figure is placed in the left foreground and is balanced by a minute black spot far

in the right background. Observe how unity is secured. Although there are a number of objects upon which the interest might be centered, we are first of all concerned with the man himself. From his figure as a center our eye takes in the lamb he is carrying, follows the direction of his staff to the dog, thence to the foremost group of stragglers, next to the misty background with its suggestion of the sea, and back again to the foreground. How smoothly the line of interest encircles the composition, yet all the while holding the central figure in the chief place. Note the contrast in the leading lines. The single, vertical line of the main figure in action relieves the monotony of the horizontal lines which predominate, and suggests a slow, dignified progress along the path.

The predominance of the horizontal lines signifies quiet and repose. In the painting of the sheep we have a good illustration of perspective. Those nearest us are represented in comparative detail, while the remaining members of the flock have less and less character as they recede from the foreground. A few strokes, suggestive only, suffice in representing the leaders of the flock.

4. **Center of Interest.** Our interest centers in the shepherd. His figure is emphasized by its position and size, by the subordination of all other objects, and by the lighting. How suggestive his form is. It speaks eloquently of gentleness, humility, industry, devotion to duty, and trustworthiness.

5. **Supreme Motive.** Determine this for yourself.

6. **Light and Color.** The highest light is on the backs of the sheep, but it is often the custom of painters to emphasize the center of interest by making it the darkest spot of the picture and arranging it against the principal light. Note that the figure of the man is given bulk and solidity as well as shape when brought up against the high light. "The tints of autumn are on every side, and a cool gray cloudy evening sky is above."

7. **Location.** The picture hangs in the Metropolitan Museum of Art, New York City, the gift of Mr. George I. Seney, 1887. Size, twenty-six inches high, thirty-seven and one-half inches wide.

QUESTIONS

What do you see first in this picture? Where is the shepherd going? Is he leading the sheep? Who is watching them? Is the shepherd an old or a young man? How does the artist show this? What is he carrying in his arms? What do you suppose has happened to it? Does his care for the little lamb show any trait of character in the shepherd? What is the expression of the dog? Of what does he seem to be thinking? What good qualities does he reveal in this scene? Of what do you suppose the good shepherd is thinking? The sheep? What is the one impression which the flock gives? What are some of the traits of a flock of sheep? What are the pleasing qualities of sheep? Can you see them all with equal distinctness? Why not? What is the expression of the old man's figure? In which are you most interested, the landscape, the sheep, or the man? Why? What season of the year is represented in this picture? How do you know? What time of day? How does the artist show this? What one thing is the artist trying to tell us in this picture? What thoughts do you have as you study it? What are the points of beauty in the scene? What do you like most about the picture?

> O Autumn! why so soon
> Depart the hues that make the forest glad,
> Thy gentle mind and thy fair sunny noon,
> And leave thee wild and sad!
>
> Ah! 'twere a lot too blest
> Forever in thy colored shade to stray;
> Amid the kisses of the soft southwest
> To rave and dream of aye,
>
> And leave the vain low strife
> That makes men mad—the tug for wealth and power—
> The passions and the cares that wither life,
> And waste its little hour.
>
> —Bryant, *Autumn Woods*

THE ARTIST

Mauve, *Mōv,* **Anton** (1838—1888), a celebrated painter of the Dutch School, was born at Zaandam, Holland. He was for a time a pupil of the cattle painter Vanos, but was chiefly self-taught. He passed most of his life at The Hague and in the village of Laren. He ranks with Israels and Maris, foremost among modern Dutch painters. ''He selected subjects similar to those painted by Millet, but he was more poetical, if less dramatic, and he was the better colorist of the two.''

Mauve usually sees the light diffused, and softly refracted here and there by figure or tree, and by his treatment of it, as it brightens the sky and floods his landscapes of silvery gray or autumn yellow browns, he gains a very beautiful atmospheric effect.

And it is just because he is not trying to paint portraits of sheep or cattle but wants to show the *effect* of a lovely spring or fall day, with the animals as they appeared to him very truly an intimate and integral part of the scene, that he is one of the greatest painters of sheep and cattle the world has known.—Greenshields

A DISTINGUISHED MEMBER OF THE HUMANE SOCIETY

Landseer

We have not to gain his confidence or his friendship: he is born our friend; while his eyes are still closed, already he believes in us: even before his birth, he has given himself to man. But the word "friend" does not exactly depict his affectionate worship. He loves us and reveres us as though we had drawn him out of nothing. He is, before all, our creature full of gratitude and more devoted than the apple of our eye. He is our intimate and impassioned slave, whom nothing repels, whose ardent trust and love nothing can impair.—Maurice Maeterlinck, *Our Friend the Dog*

THE PICTURE

One day a little girl went to the seashore to gather shells. A fine Newfoundland dog that always followed her everywhere went with her to see that no harm came to his young mistress. It was a stormy afternoon. The wind lashed the waves into foam. Suddenly a great gust swept the shore and the child, who had ventured too near the water, was caught in a great wave and carried out to sea. Quick as a flash the dog leaped in and, seizing her arm, dragged her to the shore.

Not many years ago a great ship was driven by a storm upon some rocks not far from the shore. The waves dashed furiously against the vessel, and the sailors on board knew they must perish if help did not soon reach them.

At length a gentleman with a great Newfoundland dog came upon the beach. Hearing the cries of the shipwrecked men, he gave the animal a stick and urged him toward the ship. The dog leaped into the sea and pushed through the dashing waves. The sailors understood the man's action, and when

37

he was near the ship a rope was thrown to the dog. Dropping his stick, the brave creature seized the rope and turned back. Eager hands grasped the rope when he brought it to shore and made it fast. Then the sailors by holding to it were able one by one to reach the land. Thus did a brave dog save a whole ship's crew.

Hundreds of true stories are told of dogs whose brave deeds on land and sea have made them favorites everywhere. The Newfoundland dog is brave, strong and intelligent, and the good deeds of this dog are numbered by the thousand.

Whether as the gentle protector and playfellow of boys and girls, or as the faithful companion of man, this handsome type is petted and loved by old and young, rich and poor. And why not? Does not the Newfoundland combine the most gentle, lovable disposition with a strength and courage that performs with equal ardor humble deeds and acts of real heroism?

A great painter of England, who lived not many years ago, thought so. For when Sir Edwin Landseer wished to give a message of "sympathy, kindliness and trust," he chose for the subjects of his pictures those that best revealed the fine traits of the dog.

It has been said that Landseer discovered the real dog. He knew dogs as faithful beasts of burden—the sled dogs of Newfoundland—and as the reliable messengers of the city. Their lovable traits of faithfulness and constancy to man he early learned, while the stories of their heroic acts as savers of human life deeply impressed him. Can we wonder then that his pictures which reveal this perfect understanding of the dog became at once the most popular of his time?

One day while on one of his accustomed walks through the city, Landseer met a very large and handsome Newfoundland dog carrying a basket of flowers. The beauty of the animal, for he was snow white, delighted the artist. Then, too, the fine creature paused and returned his caress with a look so full of gratitude that Landseer determined to know more about him.

Imagine his surprise when he found the dog's owner to be

A DISTINGUISHED MEMBER OF THE HUMANE SOCIETY.— *Landseer*

one of his own personal friends. It was while being enter-
tained at the home of Mr. Newman Smith near London that
the painter became personally acquainted with handsome Paul
Pry, the especial pride and delight of his master's household.
Should a portrait of the dog be painted? Yes, indeed!
Mr. Smith was only too glad to have the famous painter do
this. Accordingly the next day found Paul Pry, his handsome
coat brushed until it shone, on his way to Landseer's home.
There, upon a table in the studio, he posed with much patience
and dignity.

What a fine idea this simple scene represents. How easy it
is to read the story which the artist would have us know. A
large Newfoundland dog is resting upon a smooth block of
stone at the seaside. A gray sky, where

Anon, with flapping wings and stormy threat,
Foul seagulls came, and screamed along the coast,

is the back ground against which the form of the animal stands
out strong and lifelike. That is all. But was ever more faithful
devotion to duty pictured?

Brave, strong, intelligent, this dog poses as a member of a
life-saving society. Early on a bright summer morning he has
taken his accustomed place here at the edge of the water.
Now with the rippling, silvery wavelets lapping gently at his
feet he watches far out over the sea.

How alert he is. Those great eyes full of kindliness, sympathy and interest sweep the sea with such rapt attention that
his purpose is seen at a glance. We are made to feel in every
line of his strong, proud body that human life depends upon
his watchfulness.

What a distinguished fellow he is. See the fine snow-white
coat and great black head. How skilfully his splendid coat is
painted. It is as if we might feel the velvety softness of the
pure white hair. Here about the head magic strokes have left
it fine and silky, in fine contrast with the coarser coat on chest
and legs. His fore paws hang over the edge and are suggestive
of his readiness to leap into the water at an instant's notice.

What a noble countenance. What thoughtful eyes. Far out

on the ocean his gaze is fixed, while the attitude of his whole
body accords with the direction of his interest. The mouth is
open, displaying the powerful jaws, while the tongue projects
in response to deep, regular breathing.
See the strength shown in the broad chest and the powerful
limbs. Picture to yourself the great body in action. A drown-
ing child or a shipwrecked crew need only to signal. Not for
an instant will this dog hesitate to plunge into the ocean.
Other dogs can swim, says one, but none so willingly or so
well as the Newfoundland. In this splendid creature we have a
type which does not fail to rescue. His record is convincing.

Proudly conscious of his important charge, the noble animal
regards the whole world with a dignity not to be mistaken.
The perfect understanding on the part of the artist is shown
in every line of the figure. When Landseer was but a lad a
lady once asked him how he came to know so much about dogs
and he replied, "By peeping into their hearts, madam."

Let sympathy and kindness be shown him and this noble
creature will repay it with a love that thinks no sacrifice too
great. Through life he will remain one's most constant companion, and he has been known to die from sorrow and starva-
tion upon his master's grave. Is not this, then, the real
message the artist would convey to us?

PLAN FOR STUDY

1. **Source of Subject.** Paul Pry, a Newfoundland dog owned
by the late John Newman Smith, of Croydon, London, is the
subject. The story of the picture is told in the preceding pages.

2. **Setting.** A gray sky for a background with the faintest
suggestion of land on the left, and a stone pier in the foreground, comprise the setting. The sea and a suggestion of
foul weather indicate somewhat the idea of the subject. Note
the significance of the mooring ring, an important detail in the
setting. The few sea gulls circling restlessly against a darkening sky add to the portent of an approaching storm. These
details point with fine effect to the humane mission of the dog,
on the lookout for any catastrophe at sea.

3. **Arrangement.** The dog resting quietly on the last step is made very prominent by his enormous size and the exclusion of all other details. Observe the strength and lifelikeness of the figure—the impression of repose combined with tenseness and alertness. Note how the great eyes full of interest look out over the sea in rapt attention, and the significance of the paws overhanging the water's edge. The horizontal lines which predominate—the line of the pier, repeated in the distant horizon and in the lines of the sky—give the feeling of repose and even of solemnity. There is little or no action in the scene, but a broad suggestion of what would follow, should an alarm be sounded, is given in the alert attitude of the chief figure.

4. **Center of Interest.** The dog is the center of interest. His size in proportion to the space, the absence of any other feature in the setting his arrangement in the immediate foreground, the lighting, and the title all indicate this. The nobility of the Newfoundland type has been much praised both by poet and painter, but Robert Burns best describes him in the *Twa Dogs:*

> The first I'll name, they ca'd him Caesar,
> Was keepet for His Honor's pleasure;
> His hair, his size, his mouth, his lugs,
> Shew'd he was nane o' Scotland's dogs,
>
> . . . . . .
>
> His locked, letter'd, braw brass collar
> Shew'd him the gentleman and scholar.

5. **Supreme Motive.** Landseer painted dogs all his life. With this fact in mind it is not difficult to discover the motive which produced this painting and the sentiment it seeks to express. Here is pictured a type of dog which out of love for men and women, boys and girls, will brave the waves of the sea, or the blinding snows of the mountains. To catch the real sentiment of this particular picture one must study its companion print, *Saved,* where the noble creature has added to a remarkable record one more deed of heroism.

6. **Texture.** Much of the effectiveness of this artist's pictures is due to his rendering of texture. By texture in a painting is meant that quality of an object which appeals to

our sense of touch. Compare this painting with others by the same artist. Notice with what extreme care he has represented every detail of the dog's coat, and how the silky hair of the head is distinguished from the coarser portions.

7. Light and Shade. That the sun is well up in the sky is indicated by the shadow cast by the head. Note the play of light on the dog's coat, observing that by means of light and shade the fine effect of the hair is rendered. The brightest light falls on the chest and nose. The darkness of the sky serves to emphasize the lighter portions of the dog's body brought up against it.

8. History. This picture was painted for Mr. Newman Smith in 1838 and exhibited in the Royal Academy, London, the same year. The owner later bequeathed it to the National Gallery in 1887. The artist received $400 for the picture. At auction sales, however, Landseer's pictures brought many times that sum. *Monarch of the Glen,* for instance, sold for $36,225 in 1892. Later, engravers enlarged the head of the dog in a separate picture and named it *My Dog.*

COMMENT

He may be said to have discovered the dog. Landseer has made him the companion of man, an adjunct of human society, the generous friend and true comrade who is the last mourner at the shepherd's grave. Landseer first studied his noble countenance and his thoughtful eyes, and in so doing opened a new province to art.—Muther

In some respects it (A Distinguished Member of the Humane Society) is worthy of being deemed his masterpiece. . . . Dignified in its truth to nature, it is free from the blemish of being humanised and over-realized. It is entirely dog-like in character, its nobility and sentiment notwithstanding.—Mag. of Art

QUESTIONS

What is this picture about? What is the dog doing? Why is he here? What is the expression in his eyes? Where is the dog resting? What kind of a dog is it? What are the noble traits of this type? Why is it such a large dog? At what does he seem to be looking? What does the large ring on the pier suggest to you? What are those birds flying about? Do they seem excited? Why, do you suppose? What suggestion do they bring with them? What would be the effect if they were left out? What is the center of interest? What reason can you give for your answer? What time of day is it? Where is the sun? What are the points of beauty in the dog? What feelings do you have as you study this picture? What one thing is the artist trying to say in this picture? Does he say it plainly? What is the general impression given in the attitude of the dog? Does this picture tell you anything about the character of the artist?

There is in every animal's eye a dim image and gleam of humanity, a flash of strange light through which their life looks out and up to our great mystery of command over them, and claims the fellowship of the creature, if not the soul.—Ruskin

THE ARTIST

Land'seer, Sir Edwin Henry (1802—1873), an English animal painter of renown, was born in London, where he spent the greater part of his life. His father was a well-known engraver and writer on art. Edwin received his early training from his father and at an early age attained great skill in drawing animals and humorous sketches. When he was but thirteen, one of his sketches was exhibited in the Royal Academy. At fourteen he became a student in the Royal Academy, and at twenty-nine he was taken into full membership.

Landseer established his studio in St. John's Row, London, where all of his famous pictures were painted. He visited Scotland in 1824, and repeated his visit annually for a number of years. His deer pictures were the chief result of these visits. He was knighted in 1850. Between 1809 and 1873 he painted over 630 pictures, many of which are in the South Kensington Museum and the Royal Art Gallery, London.

He was one of the greatest animal painters the world has ever known.

His life was healthy, vigorous, and breezy.—Sweetser

He won all hearts by his genial disposition, gentle manners, and distinct personal charm.—Masters in Art No. 5.

SHOEING THE BAY MARE

Landseer

Under a spreading chestnut-tree
The village smithy stands;
The smith, a mighty man is he,
With large and sinewy hands;
And the muscles of his brawny arms
Are strong as iron bands.

His hair is crisp, and black, and long,
His face is like the tan;
His brow is wet with honest sweat,
He earns whate'er he can,
And looks the whole world in the face,
For he owes not any man.

—Longfellow, *The Village Blacksmith*

THE PICTURE

It was near the close of a bright October day. Down an avenue of fine old elm trees already touched with the red and gold of autumn, a gentleman was slowly walking. A youth who stood waiting some distance ahead interested him.

"I am a stranger here in Cambridge," was the lad's greeting. "I landed in Boston only yesterday; my home is across the ocean. Could you tell me, please," he added earnestly, "where I might find that chestnut tree which Mr. Longfellow tells about in his poem of the blacksmith?"

Surprised and delighted, the gentleman, who was Thomas Wentworth Higginson, answered, "Indeed, I can only show you where it stood, for it is no longer there. It was cut down years ago. And do you know, my boy," he exclaimed proudly, "I was one of those children who 'looked in at the open door' myself!"

45

It was indeed a strange pair who stood a few minutes later in another quiet street of the village. Silently they were looking at the spot which the gentleman pointed out. Happy with a great desire fulfilled, the youth spoke:

"Mr. Longfellow's *Village Blacksmith* was the first poem I ever read in my school books. Every time I recited it I promised myself that if I ever visited this country I would come here first of all to see that old chestnut tree. And oh," he exclaimed with eyes sparkling, "I am so glad I'm here!"

Does not this boy from a far-off country voice the sentiments of school children everywhere? Would not we joyfully welcome the opportunity to visit this same spot to do honor to the poet who gave us its delightful story? But what shall we say of the painter who has sketched a similar smithy in this charming picture before us? How fitting it is that this message of the blacksmith's toil should live also on an artist's canvas.

Strange as it may seem, Edwin Landseer, the most popular painter of England, in the very same year that the poet of Cambridge wrote his poem, described a similar scene in a great picture. In 1844 when a wealthy friend asked him to sketch a portrait of a favorite horse, a shoeing scene was selected.

Years before, when this same pet was but a frisky foal, the proud owner had shown her to the artist. He desired then that a sketch of her be made. But years had passed since that time, years of busy days for the artist. Pictures of dogs, of lions, and of graceful deer had crowded out all thoughts of the foal, which had grown very beautiful under the care of a fond master.

Betty, for that was the foal's name, had developed certain well-defined habits of her own. She insisted on standing at all times without halter or rope. Under no circumstances would she consent to be tied to post or barn door. But the most unusual habit of all was her occasional trip to the forge. All alone she would trot to this place when new shoes were needed.

It was at the time of one of these trips that the artist

SHOEING THE BAY MARE.—*Landseer*

chanced to be with Mr. Bell, the owner of Betty. Imagine his
surprise when he saw her come trotting home. It was not the
Betty of bygone days, but an intelligent bay mare which the
artist now saw.

"I am determined to paint Betty after all," he exclaimed
to Mr. Bell. The next day found her established, to her own
great satisfaction, in the country blacksmith shop. Imagine
Mr. Bell's delight when this charming picture was presented
to him.

May not we, too, share his enjoyment? Come, let us enter
through this door into the quaint little shop. The "roaring
bellows" and "flaming forge" are all here. With its stone
floor and solid brick walls, the room is unlike any of the
smithies we have seen in our own country. So very small is it
that the family group within must find it very difficult to
move about. The building must be old, for here and there the
plaster has fallen. To the right is seen a part of the forge,
while the necessary tools are placed handily in the foreground.

How perfectly at home the animals seem. With what interest
they watch the shoeing. Betty, with arching neck and shapely
head, with its pure white star, looks as if she would speak.
Perfectly at home, she stands between anvil and forge in a
space that is scarcely large enough for her.

How small and shaggy and humble seems the little donkey
looking out from under Betty's neck. How finely contrasted
is the meek and patient bearing of the donkey with that of the
high-spirited mare. Surprising to behold, she stands without
halter of any kind. Amazed at such an unheard-of thing,
critics promptly said that such a condition was not true. But
we who know Betty's habits are quite certain that the artist
painted her just as she appeared. Did she not come to the
shop this very day of her own accord?

Laura, the bloodhound, another interested member of the
group, rests quietly somewhat apart from the others. A pet
of Mr. Bell's, she often comes with the bay mare to this shop.
With head well forward, long ears drooping, and now and
then sniffing the odors, her eyes are fixed intently upon the
shoeing.

To the right, with body braced for the task in hand, the smith holds the mare's hoof in his rough leather apron, while he fits the shoe. It is this simple, honest labor that is the keynote of the charming scene. True it is that Betty holds our interest, but it is the industry, the act of shoeing which the artist has made the central idea.

Is not the whole arrangement, the very atmosphere of the little shop filled with its sound? Betty turns with questioning look to watch the work. Although the donkey cannot see the act his head turns in that direction, while his ears move gently in an effort to catch the sound. The whole attitude of the smith is that of one absorbed in his task. Follow a line from Betty's face, along the donkey's head, over the dog's nose, and parallel with the tools in the box and we find ourselves with the act itself.

The shoeing is well advanced. By dint of shaping them when glowing hot on the anvil nearby, the shoes have been fitted one at a time, and placed on the bench at the right.

At this stage of the process the little shop must have looked most attractive. It was at such a time as this when the roaring bellows and the ringing blows were sending out showers of sparks that the Cambridge

> Children coming from school
> Looked in at the open door;
> They love to see the flaming forge,
> And hear the bellows roar,
> And catch the burning sparks that fly
> Like chaff from a threshing-floor.
>
> —Longfellow

Now with tools at hand the smith is trying the shoe to Betty's foot. So natural is the action that we may almost see the downward movement of the hoof and the man carrying the shoe to the forge.

It is this honest toil of the cheery, manly blacksmith that called forth the poet's praise. Has not the artist, too, made it the lesson of this scene? Among these gentle friends of the fields he seems content with his daily task. That he loves these dumb creatures is shown by their confidence in him. Even the cage in the light of the doorway holds little friends who sing their message of good cheer all day long.

Thanks, thanks to thee, my worthy friend,
For the lesson thou has taught!
Thus at the flaming forge of life
Our fortunes must be wrought;
Thus on its sounding anvil shaped
Each burning deed and thought!

—Longfellow

PLAN FOR STUDY

1. Source of Subject. The preceding pages contain the story of the picture. Tradition has it that the kindly old blacksmith of this scene was Mr. Jacob Bell himself.

2. Setting. A quaint country blacksmith shop. Here are found all the tools and objects commonly found in such a place—the kit placed handily in the foreground, a bench, a suggestion of the forge in the right foreground, and a number of shoes. The great width of wall as seen through the doorway, and the small working space suggest the possibility of the shop's being located in some deserted building. The details are carefully worked out. Observe the little cage swinging cheerfully in the sunshine of the open door and its general effect, the characteristic garb of the blacksmith—leather apron, and work shirt with sleeves rolled up and collar unbuttoned.

3. Arrangement. The arrangement is somewhat circular. The mare, because of her position and size, dominates the scene, while the comparatively smaller figures of the man, donkey and bloodhound are skilfully distributed so as to balance the arrangement in the foreground, and at the same time not detract from the central figure. Note how pleasing the arrangement of the figures can be in so small a space. There is no impression of crowding, nor of inconvenience.

Observe how the center of interest is strongly emphasized by the leading lines. Starting with the figure of the mare, we follow a line over her shapely neck and head, thence along the head of the donkey, over the dog's nose, and, finally, following the direction of the tools in the box and the arm of the smith, we are at the very act of shoeing. The line is then taken up along the left arm of the smith and carried around the curved form of the mare, circling the whole composition. Observe the effect of the open doorway, other than admitting light to the shop. This glimpse out of doors serves to add a touch of freedom to the otherwise cramped quarters of the picture.

Study the variety and the significance of the lines. The dominating curved lines of Betty's back, the bent figure of the smith, the neck of the donkey, and the rounded back of the bloodhound are relieved by the perpendicular lines of the doorway, the walls, and the smaller objects, and by the horizontal lines of the floor, the door, the bench and the tool-kit. Note the sense of repose and how this feeling is conveyed by the listening attitude of the animals. True enough, the sounds of shoeing fill the air, but then they are not discordant. The points of beauty and intelligence in the bay mare, the sturdy, manly, kindly qualities of the smith, the evident humility and patient attitude of the donkey and the characteristic pose of the bloodhound are worthy of careful study.

4. **Center of Interest.** The artist places the greatest emphasis on the act of shoeing. The title might suggest that this was the center of interest; but the artist uses stronger methods. In the arrangement we saw that the strongest lines lead to the act. But the chief method used here is the interest of the principal figures. Note that the horse turns questioningly in the direction of the sound, the donkey seeks to locate it and listens intently, the bloodhound looks directly into the smith's hands, while he himself is absorbed in his work. Then, too, the whole scene is filled with the sound and odor of the industry. Note also the effect of the lighting in emphasizing the center of interest.

5. **Light and Shade.** We have repeatedly noticed that the shape and solidity of objects in a composition are affected by the light and shade. The reality of this scene is largely due to the effective handling of the light which enters through the open doorway. We see at once the significance of limiting its entrance to the upper half of the picture, otherwise there could

be no gradations of light in the lower portions. Note how the strongest dark of Betty's figure is brought up against the highest light, and the effect of this arrangement. The little touch of light in the right background serving to round out that portion of her form against it might be attributed to the blaze on the forge, were it not for an established rule that a picture shall have but one principal light. The note of freshness, of cheery warmth which the light gives adds much to the charm of the picture. The beautiful play of light on the rounded figure of the mare makes the glossy coat fairly brilliant in spots.

6. **Texture.** The painstaking care of the artist is shown in the skill with which the quality of the leather in the apron, the details of the tools and box, the curly hair of smith, the sleek coat of the bloodhound, and the wood of the bird cage and the shagginess of the donkey's coat in contrast to the glowing coat of the mare are all worked out.

7. **Supreme Motive.** Landseer's supreme motive seemed to be to show, through the medium of dumb animals, the goodwill, kindly sympathy, optimism and faith of his own pure nature. We cannot help thinking that in this scene he was inspired by the honest, cheery toil of the smith as well, while in the confidence and love which these dumb friends evinced for the shoer he undoubtedly sought to show the helpful relations that exist between man and domestic animals.

8. **History.** This picture was painted in 1844 for Mr. Jacob Bell and exhibited that same year in the National Gallery, London. A few years later Mr. Bell bequeathed it to the National Gallery, where it now hangs. Its size is four feet eight inches by three feet eight inches. The original lends itself easily to translation, that is to say, engravings made of the original, of which our own small copy is a print, are almost as effective and beautiful as the painting which hangs in the Gallery.

COMMENT

Every pose he gave to an animal, every expression of passion, or of action, every detail of hide and fur, of skin, hair, and wool, of eyes and teeth, of hoof and claw, were carefully studied from the life.

He accomplished with single strokes of a broad brush effects of detail which other artists would have had laboriously to work in, as it were, in pencil strokes.—Eaton

It is as if he had become possessed of a magic cap, with which he could draw close to animals without being observed, and surprise their nature and inmost life.—Muther

Landseer had a very real message to give to the world, a message of kindliness and compassion, of sympathy and trust; and he felt best able to give this message through the medium of his dumb friends, where other men had chosen religious subjects or broad poetic schemes.—M. Dougal Scott

QUESTIONS

What is this picture about? What is the man doing? What is his occupation? Do you know a real blacksmith? Does he look like this one? What is the expression in the mare's eyes? What is she doing? Do you think she enjoys the shoeing? How does the artist show this? What is the expression on the donkey's face? Why do you suppose he is here? How can you tell that he is listening? In what does he seem most interested? What is the dog doing? In what do all the animals seem interested? How does the artist show this? Where does the light in the picture come from? What does it add to the picture? Where does your eye rest longest in the scene? Can you point out the center of interest? What are the chief points of beauty in the bay mare? What are some of her traits of character? In what are you most interested in the picture? What is the expression on the man's face? Of what is he thinking? What other objects of interest do you see in the picture? In which are you more interested, the animals or the arrangement of the smithy? What sounds do you seem to hear? What actions do you seem to see? What are the most pleasing things about the picture? What thoughts come to you as you study it? What one thing do you think the artist is trying to tell us here? Does he tell it plainly? What good qualities of the artist does this picture reveal?

RED DEER OF CHILLINGHAM

Landseer

As chief, who hears his warder call,
'To arms! the foemen storm the wall,'
The antlered monarch of the waste
Sprung from his heathery couch in haste.
But ere his fleet career he took,
The dew-drops from his flank he shook;
Like crested leader proud and high
Tossed his beamed frontlet to the sky;
A moment gazed adown the dale,
A moment snuffed the tainted gale,
A moment listened to the cry,
That thickened as the chase drew nigh.

—Sir Walter Scott, *Lady of the Lake*

THE PICTURE

In the valley of the river Till in northern England stands the ancient castle of Chillingham. On all sides hills and moorland stretch in unbroken solitude to the confines of the great estate, where the famous red deer and wild cattle roam at will.

It was during that period in the history of the estate when Lord Ossulston had succeeded to the title of Earl of Tankerville, owner of Chillingham Castle, that Sir Edwin Landseer was a guest. Some years before he had chanced to visit the earl on a tour through Northumberland. He had never forgotten the bracing climate, the glorious scenery and the freedom of the Highlands. Then, too, he had begun a study of the life and habits of the red deer, the native deer of north England and the object of the chase.

It was the morning of the hunt. Just when the faintest streaks of light were to be seen in the east, a company of men, Sir Edwin among them, rode silently out of the castle gate.

54

RED DEER OF CHILLINGHAM.—*Landseer*

All carried the formidable weapons of the chase. A chill air set their blood atingle, and a sharp breeze brought them the fresh odors of the forest. A glad note of exhilaration caught the spirits of the men, and they pushed forward with the keenest anticipation.

In another portion of the estate a group of the hunted tarried unsuspectingly in a secluded spot. A magnificent stag and his mate were feeding quietly upon the tender shoots and leaves, and a little fawn was asleep near by. Ever and anon the father lifted his head and sniffed the air. The trust of the mother in his protection was complete and the sleeping fawn seemed her only interest.

Suddenly the stag looked up with a quick, startled expression. The mother turned and leaped nimbly to where the fawn lay sleeping. She, too, stood alert, her sensitive nose turned in the direction from which the scent came, her ears lifted to catch the faintest sound. The fawn awakened with a start. The mother stood over it protectingly, never for an instant relaxing her watchful attitude. For a single moment they paused, not quite certain in which direction to flee.

Far enough away not to be observed, but yet near enough to see this pretty spectacle, Sir Edwin studied the group with keen delight. His gun had been thrown aside. With quick, vigorous strokes he was sketching the deer while his companions, disgusted with the apparent weakness of the man, stood idly by and watched him.

With simple directness our print pictures the group at that critical moment. When we study the graceful creatures in this scene, it is not hard to appreciate the sentiment of the artist who preferred to sketch rather than to shoot them. With what a lordly manner the stag, the most prominent figure of the group, lifts his head to catch the faintest scent. Unconsciously he poses for us, and that is the secret of his beauty. See the poise of the great body. Every muscle is tense, while in the wild, questioning eyes is mirrored all the agony of suspense. The feet seem scarcely to touch the ground as the slender limbs are held for instant action. Every fiber of his being is afire with the thrilling challenge of the moment

Can one doubt the courage of this creature if he be brought to bay?

But our sympathy goes out to the defenceless members of the group. Mother love seems strongest in the moment of greatest danger. With what tenderness the artist has here touched that note. We see only the pretty spotted coat of the fawn and the reddish brown body of the mother, their legs and feet are hidden. Her head is turned in the direction of the scent, her ears are strained to catch the faintest sound and her great brown eyes are eloquent with startled mother love.

The fawn, whose slim little legs are still weak, has staggered awkwardly to her side. He leans for support against the mother and his eyes, round and soft like hers, instinctively look in the right direction. What pathos there is in their companionship! They seem so alone. The great creature so near is apparently far away in thought. To be sure, he sniffs the air with all his powers concentrated to do battle if there be need. Yet we cannot feel certain that he will do it in their defence. His record is not so convincing as that of the mother who has been known to leap into the very jaws of death that her fawn might go untouched. His is the anticipation of battle and of victory. Those mighty antlers will prove a fair defence. But the mother in this respect is defenseless. Her keen wit and her nimbleness alone, must save both her fawn and herself, if such a thing be possible.

PLAN FOR STUDY

1. **Source of Subject.** A group of red deer on the Chillingham estate, near the village of Chillingham, Northumberland, England. Lord Tankerville, the owner, and the artist were staunch friends. The red deer as a subject for his brush fascinated Landseer. The subject of this sketch was chanced upon during his second visit to the castle in 1867.

2. **Setting.** The deer are pictured in a natural landscape which we may be sure is an accurate copy of the hilly region of the Chillingham estate. This is essentially a figure picture, the landscape attracting comparatively little interest. The

vegetation is represented in detail in the foreground, perhaps
to suggest a satisfactory feeding spot. The cloudy sky is in
keeping with the thought. The "red deer lands" of northern
England and Scotland are unsuited for any other purpose than
vast grazing tracts. Only here and there in a great estate of
moorland, hill and woodland are little patches fit for cultiva-
tion. Our print is suggestive of the general character of
the region.

3. **Arrangement.** The chief figures are arranged in the foreground, while farther back to the right the watchful, anxious
attitude of the family is repeated in another group. The stag,
because of his size and position, dominates the scene, and
recalls to mind the noble *Monarch of the Glen.* Only the
bodies of the mother and fawn are seen. The effect of the
predominating vertical lines; the height of the painting as
compared to its width and the erect position of all the figures,
are in keeping with the spirit of the subject. There is also
a suggestion of variety in the slanting lines of the hillside,
both in the fore- and back-ground, and the lines of the antlers.
Study the principle of perspective; observe the detail in the
grass in the foreground as compared with a mere suggestion
in the background.

Compare the detail in the nearest figures with the suggestive
touches of the brush which represent the animals farther back.
The unstudied pose of the chief figures gives to the picture its
greatest charm. The artist has instinctively caught them
when their most characteristic traits are revealed. We must
not fail to recognize always this quality of Landseer's pictures.

4. **Center of Interest.** The stag is the center of interest.
Show how the artist emphasizes this fact.

5. **Light and shade.** Again we find the artist's characteristic attention given to representing the coats of his animals.
The play of light brings out their full beauty. Note the light
on the head of the mother which brings out every line of her
sensitive face, and how the white neck of the fawn is brought
up against the dark of the mother's body. Observe the fine
distinction in rendering the coat of the stag, the silky hair
of ears and head as distinguished from the coarser portions.

6. **Supreme Motive.** Landseer was particularly touched by the tragic element in the deer's existence. Says one:

> In almost all of his heads of deer there is an expression of sensitiveness, grandeur and pain, as if he foreshadowed their fate, and pitied them from the depths of his heart. . . . The deer so grand in his isolation, so gentle and graceful, so valiant and strong, is never approached by man except as a destroyer, and all its fascinations and noble traits are held only at the mercy of the rifle ball. . . . Valor, strength, and thought of humanity are seen in their disguise, in their conflicts, flights and saddening fate.

This element seems especially strong in this picture, yet it is not overdrawn. These are true animals of the woods, their natural instincts are not masked by sentiment. Herein lies the true worth of the picture.

7. **History.** *The Red Deer of Chillingham* was painted in 1867 and exhibited the same year in the Royal Academy. It was engraved by Thomas Landseer, the artist's older brother, and many prints of the engraving have been made.

COMMENT

> Stags and roes were really first introduced into painting by Landseer. . . . Landseer's are true kings of the forest, the shooting of which ought to be punished as an act of assassination. . . . With what a bold spirit they raise their heads to sniff the mountain air, whilst their antlers show their delight in battle and the joy of victory. . . . How gentle and timid is the noble, defenceless roe in Landseer's pictures!—Muther

> Beneath a hill whose rocky side
> O'erbrowed a grassy mead
> And fenced a cottage from the wind,
> A deer was wont to feed.

> The cottage dame forbade her son
> To aim the rifle here;
> ''It were a shame,'' she said, ''to harm
> Or fight that friendly deer.

> ''This spot has been my pleasant home
> Ten peaceful years and more,
> And ever when the moonlight shines
> She feeds before our door.

''The red-men say that here she walked
A thousand moons ago;
They never raise the war-whoop here,
And never twang the bow.

''I love to watch her as she feeds,
And think that all is well
While such a gentle creature haunts
The place in which we dwell.''

—Bryant, *The White-Footed Deer*

QUESTIONS

What creatures are these? Have you ever seen any? Where? What were they doing? What do you suppose has happened? What makes you think so? What is the expression on each of their faces? Is this expression the same on all their faces? What word might best describe their attitude? What are the beautiful qualities of these deer? In which are you most interested? Why? Is the little fawn afraid? In whom does it seem to have most confidence? How does it show its love for its mother? How does she show her love for the fawn? How many deer do you see in the picture? Why are not those in the background painted more distinctly? Where is the light? What does it add to the scene? What are your feelings as you study the scene? What one thing does the artist seem to be saying in this picture? What qualities of the artist does this picture reveal? What do you like best about it? In which are you most interested, the landscape or the animals? Why?

THE SPINNER

Maes

Because the sunset sky
Makes music in my soul,
Only to fail and die,
Shall I not take the whole
Of beauty that it gives
While yet it lives?

—Richard Watson Gilder

THE PICTURE

Good woman, we would know your difficulty. Your absorbed, patient air as you bend to a perplexing task appeals very strongly to us.

From the action of the fingers we conclude that the band connecting wheel and spindle has broken. Patience is about to have its reward, however, for the thread is almost mended.

See how the sunlight streams in from an opposite window and fills the room with a cheerful glow. Tenderly it touches the wrinkled forehead and the strong hands of the worker. How we are drawn to her. Her genial, comfortable presence breathes a peace and contentment without which a home is not truly a home. Crowned with the glory of a ripe, old age, when, if ever, one should have time for rest and reflection, she is still at her task.

There was a time, we may be sure, back in the sunny days when her dreams were rosy ones. Now she can contemplate them either realized or forever gone. There was a time when ambition to do big things may have come to her, but we doubt it. Hers is the type of those plain, humble folk who see duty very clearly in a lowly sphere. Back over such a life it is a blessed privilege of hers to-day to reflect.

61

Truly enough the shadowy hours may come, but still

> Good deeds they do; they comfort and they bless
> In duties others put off till the morrow;
> Their look is balm, their touch is tenderness
> To all in sorrow.

> Faithful in life, and faithful unto death,
> Such souls, in sooth, illumine with lustre splendid
> That glimpsed, glad land wherein, the Vision saith,
> Earth's wrongs are ended.

—Richard Burton

PLAN FOR STUDY

1. Source of Subject. Although Maes devoted a larger part of his life to the painting of portraits, his heart was not in that work. Simple, quiet lives in their customary scenes of labor interested him most. This picture showing a Dutch interior is representative of those pictures which, painted in his middle period, have given his works a place in the annals of true art.

2. Setting. The simplicity of the setting, and the suggestion of comfort in spite of bare walls and rough floor, give the scene a homelike atmosphere. Poverty is revealed here in almost every detail, but it is poverty of the respectable sort. The humble place of this woman in life is not due to her thriftlessness. She is merely doing the very best she knows how in the humble sphere in which circumstances have placed her. Note her comfortable dress, the neat kerchief, the customary house cap. The suggestion of repose in her figure is emphasized, perhaps, by the suggestion of strength in the chair in which she sits. The tongs resting in one corner of the broad chimney suggest a cheerful fire in the fireplace. Beside this is a cracked earthen jar. Why is the jar cracked? Why is it shown in the composition at all? Would it serve as good a purpose in another place in the room?

3. Arrangement. The arrangement is a pleasing feature of the composition. Five objects of varying degrees of interest have been so placed that the charm of the picture is irresistible.

Does this figure seem tense or re-
laxed? Point to the warm and cool
colors used in this painting. Are the
warm colors used in the foreground
or in the background? Where are
the cool colors used? When judging
this picture, to which aesthetic
qualities—literal, visual, or
expressive—did you refer most
often?

Permission Geo. P. Brown & Co.

THE SPINNER.—*Maes*

The figure of the spinner is placed behind her flax wheel. An earthen pot on the right balances the large wheel. Suspended from the wall is a reel upon which the yarn is wound when taken from the spindle. At the extreme right is a suggestion of the broad chimney with the tongs placed handily in the corner. Note how the rounded surface of the jar serves to counteract the impression of aspiration and dignity in the vertical lines of tongs and wall; also the pleasing variety of lines.

4. **Center of Interest.** The attitude of the woman and the lighting direct our attention at once to the woman's hands, whose strength and character speak eloquently of a life of service mainly for others. Do they not also give a strong suggestion of the sturdy, robust character of the woman? Aged, calloused with toil, and somewhat stiffened, they nevertheless perform their customary daily task. How completely engrossed the woman is just now! The whirring spindle is stilled, and absolute quiet reigns in the room, for its single occupant is intent upon making the wheel perform its work again.

5. **Supreme Motive.** What do you think the artist is trying to tell us in this picture? Does he tell it plainly? What does the picture tell you about the character and life of the man who painted it? Why do you suppose he painted this scene in just this way?

6. **Light and Shade.** The unusual method here employed is somewhat after the style of Rembrandt, with whom Maes studied. The light comes evidently from a high casement on the opposite side of the room and forms a pleasing feature of the composition. Aside from the cheery, warm note it adds to the scene, it brings out strongly the hands and features of the spinner as her form stands out strong and lifelike against the bright glare of the wall. Follow the light as it runs along the band connecting wheel and spindle, over the woman's dress and kerchief, along her spectacle rims and touches lightly her forehead. Note the effect of the shadow of the distaff in breaking the triangular glare upon the wall. Also the light and shadow in bringing out the crack and other

details of the earthen pot. Observe also the pleasing treatment of the shadowy portions of the room.

7. **Color.** The coloring is one of the strongest features of the picture.

It unites the subtlety of chiaroscuro, vigorous coloring, and great mastery in handling, with the true finish which never becomes trivial. Maes lights his subjects after the manner of his master (Rembrandt), but the general tone of his coloring is cooler and more silvery, notably so in this example. There is a high note of color in the rich and glowing red of the sleeves of the old woman, which illumines the whole in a delightful way, and to which, as a culminating point, the harmonies of the surrounding tints, the warm depth of the background, the yellow of the wooden floor, the brown of the spinning wheel, and the richer and deeper line of the skirt below, the brighter color of the red earthen jar, and the fine, mellow tones of the flesh all lead up. It is this final and glowing touch of red that makes the whole thing ''sing,'' to use a studio word. There is a fine touch of warm blue introduced in a bit of drapery that falls over the bench of the wheel; and the whites of the apron and of the kerchief about the neck are of a very fine neutral shade in the half-lights.—T. Cole

8. **History.** This picture, painted on wood in that period in which Maes produced those of his pictures which alone have stood the test of true art, hangs in the Vander Hoop collection in Ryks Museum, Amsterdam. Size, sixteen and one-quarter inches high and thirteen and three-eighths inches wide. In the same gallery there is another picture of an old woman spinning which was painted by Maes and is somewhat larger than this we are studying. Both are equally admired.

COMMENT

No master has portrayed old age with greater charm and suggestion of content.—Zug

I like the action of the figure—its absorbed attentiveness, so simple, natural, and unaffected. Here we see an experienced Dutch housewife—a robust and beautiful old woman and a type of her kind; one of those kind, hale, thrifty souls whose mere presence breathes a sense of homeliness and serenity.—T. Cole

It pleased Maes to paint aged women, sometimes seated at the table before a frugal repast, for which they give thanks to God; sometimes seated before their spinning wheel whereby to gain their livelihood.—Bredius

QUESTIONS

What is this picture about? Have you ever seen a real spinning wheel? Where? What is this woman doing just now? What seems to be the trouble? What is she spinning? From what is linen made? Have you ever seen flax growing in a field? What does it look most like? How is it prepared for the spinning wheel? For the loom? What is this bundle of it on the distaff called? What is the expression on the woman's face? Of what is she thinking? Is she patient or vexed at this moment? Why do you think so? What is the most pleasing quality she evidently possesses? What other good qualities of character do you think she has? What made you think of them? Do you note anything unusual about her hands. What impression do they give? What other objects do you see in the room? What is the general impression which you get from the picture? How is comfort suggested? Contentment? Quiet? Poverty? Respectability? Tidiness? Repose? What does the glimpse of the tongs add? What purpose does the earthen jar serve? What would be the effect if it were left out? What does it suggest to you? What unusual thing do you observe about the lighting? Where does it come from? Is it pleasing? Why? What different kinds of lines do you see? Which lines predominate? What effect does this have in the picture? What is the artist trying to tell us in the picture? Does he tell it plainly? What does the picture tell us about the life and character of the man who painted it? Where is the center of interest? What thoughts do you have as you study the picture? Does it appeal to the eye or to the feeling? What are the most pleasing things about it?

> Labor is rest, from the sorrows that greet us;
> Rest from the petty vexations that meet us;
> 　Rest from world-sirens that lure us to ill.
> Work—and pure slumbers shall wait on thy pillow;
> Work—thou shalt ride over Care's coming billow;
> Lie not down wearied 'neath Woe's weeping willow;
> 　Work with stout heart and resolute will.
>
> **Frances S. Osgood**

THE ARTIST

Maes, *Maas,* **Nicholas** (1632—1693), a Dutch painter, was born at Dordrecht. At the age of eighteen he entered Rembrandt's school in Amsterdam and was strongly influenced by this master of light and shadow. His first paintings were of subjects in common life, and are his best works. In 1660 he went to Antwerp, where he became a portrait painter. Maes was so close a follower of Rembrandt in his style that some of his pictures are credited to his great teacher. He is represented in the museums of Amsterdam and Berlin; in the Louvre, Paris; in the National Gallery, London; and in many private collections, especially in England.

Of all Rembrandt's pupils, he was perhaps the most successful in the management of light.

THE SONG OF THE LARK
Breton

I have walked through wilderness dreary
And to-day my heart is weary;
Had I now the wings of a fairy,
Up to thee would I fly.
There is madness about thee, and joy divine
In that song of thine;
Lift me, guide me, high and high
To thy banqueting place in the sky.

—Wordsworth

THE PICTURE

Just when the softest glow and faintest streaks of dawn were touching the eastern sky, this strong young woman came out from her humble home to begin her day's toil in the fields. With the glory of the new day stirring her soul, she has heard the song of the lark. Her face is upturned as she follows its flight, her form straightens unconsciously in response to the happy thoughts the bird inspires within her.

A sickle, suggestive of the grass she must cut the livelong day, is clasped firmly in one hand, the other hangs idly at her side. The sleeves of her waist are rolled up, revealing the rounded arms that have known the most wearisome toil. Her collar is made low for comfort. The familiar headdress of the French peasant woman holds back the heavy braids from her face. A short woolen skirt and an apron doubled and fastened to hold the gleanings complete her costume.

There is little of care or sorrow in the fresh young face, just now so joyously uplifted. It is as if her spirit responded happily to the drudgery of her task in such an environment. Care, worry, disappointment, privation—all are forgotten as she listens to the song of the bird. Hers is an untutored knowledge of nature. Daily toil, only, has brought her in closest association with birds, grass and flowers.

68

THE SONG OF THE LARK.—*Breton*

Still the bird sings on. The girl's lips unconsciously repeat its notes, even as her eyes follow its flight. Higher and higher each bright gleam of color shoots above the horizon until at last the whole eastern heavens are aflame with the ruddy glow. Now the sun itself peeps above the trees and roofs, and the drowsy world takes on new life.

Delicate flowers, wet with dew, lift their heads at her feet. Midsummer breezes bring the dainty perfume of flower and shrub. A thousand sounds of the awakened earth blend into the sweet melody that comes with the sunrise. A simple, uncultured, hard-working girl of the open country, her soul is fairly lifted out of itself as she responds to the beauty and wonders of the great world about her. For a passing moment only, is her rude labor touched with the warmest colors, even as her whole being is purified by this brief glimpse into the mysteries and glories of creation.

Sing on, heaven-born bird! The girl still listens, enraptured, to your song, her thoughts as pure as the morning itself.

> And drown'd in yonder living blue
> The lark becomes a sightless song.

PLAN FOR STUDY

1. **Source of Subject.** The fields of Artois furnished many subjects for Breton's paintings, one of these being the original of our print. The artist in his Autobiography relates in a most charming way his own impressions of this scene:

Oh, joy! joy of the eyes, joy of the soul! reconciliation of the individual with himself in the outpouring of universal love! I luxuriated in all the effluence of life—of nature—the effervescent life of plants wet with the morning dew, the waving of the grain in the morning breeze, the rapturous song of the larks heralding the dawn; flaming poppies, modest corn-flowers, mysterious distances fading into the peaceful sky, odors that waken ecstatic thrills, intoxicating emanations, radiance of free, pure light. . . . Oh, divine charm! Oh, all-bountiful God, revealing thyself to the heart through so many ineffable blessings!

2. **Setting.** The setting has all the charm of a Millet subject with, perhaps, the added charm of an artist who with poetic instinct painted the most beautiful features of the open coun-

try. The girl in her humble attire is the absorbing feature in the landscape. In the sickle we find the suggestion of her mission. The depth of sky makes a very important contribution to the general impression. The suggestion of the village at the edge of the field, the path the girl has traversed, the broad sun above the eastern horizon, all reveal the story of this morning's walk. The impression of absolute repose and stillness is broken only by the harmony of morning sounds in which the song of the lark rings out clear and strong.

3. **Arrangement.** The chief figure is silhouetted against a deep sky and field. The predominating horizontal lines are expressive of strength and rest. Note how effectively the details have been subordinated, how quickly they are grasped, even as we contemplate the attitude of the listening girl. Here the landscape, by every poetic instinct, is made charming to the eye, but note in how small a measure, if any, it tends to detract from the central thought. Note the blurred character of the foliage through the atmosphere, the detail in the grass and flowers at the girl's feet, contrasted with the suggestive shrubs and trees in the middle distance and background. Observe the strength of the figure, the suggestion of space behind it, the strong modeling of feet and arms, and the simplicity of the clothing.

4. **Center of Interest.** While the figure of the girl, because of its prominent position and size, is the one absorbing feature of the composition, the lark itself is the center of our interest. The attention of the girl thrilled with its song is fixed upon the lark.

5. **Texture.** An eminent art critic makes the following comment on the texture:

Flesh is here represented as it should be in all the glow and flush of a young healthy life. The color and textures are as they appear in nature. The scratch of a cornstalk upon the cheeks will not tear them open; nor the sickle edge of the stubble cut the bare brown feet. There is pliability, strength and endurance in such flesh.

6. **Supreme Motive.** The supreme motive of the artist seems to be to idealize the life of the French peasant. Millet and Breton are invariably compared. Both loved nature, both rep-

resented the peasant workers in the fields. But here the analogy stops. Both were inspired by entirely different mo tives. Said Millet in comparing his work with that of Breton, "We are both seeking infinite nature. We are free to follow the furrow which we love, preferring, you, the convolvulus in the wheat and I the rude potatoes." Again in conversation with Breton, he said, "Why should not painters have the right to choose, one, the rough potato, the other, the morning-glory that twines itself among the corn?" With characteristic directness Millet thus points out the essential difference between them.

The world, although much impressed with the latter's pic- tures, which always command high prices, has accorded to the former the master's place. Breton was a poet, not a peasant. Millet was peasant, not a poet, save only to that degree in which he expressed the beauty of the commonplace, and the harmony between the worker and his task. Breton lived in the city, he visited the country. Millet lived in the country, he abhorred the city and the superficial character of existence there. Breton had never toiled in the fields, Millet from a youth up had bent to his task under a scorching sun. One was born in a sunny region in a comfortable home, the other passed his boyhood in the bracing atmosphere of the bleak Normandy coast, nurtured in a peasant home.

Breton in his walks through the fields sang as he walked, noted the pleasant and the beautiful features, ignoring the lowly and ugly. Millet—consider his experience—saw only the drudgery, the seriousness of an existence of a race which found it difficult to obtain bread, even when they did toil for it in the sweat of their brows. Beauty for him lay not in the transcendent glories of sky and field, but in the harmony between the toiler and his work, in the heroic steadfastness of the peasant type. Life was serious, nature was exacting, existence was drudgery. Breton himself recognized the mas- ter's power, for he said, "Because Millet has created master- pieces, depicting man degraded by poverty even to the efface- ment of his individuality, we have not therefore the right to deny the exalted, the divine beauty of these masterpieces."

Breton's pictures, then, reflect his own attitude. They appeal to the eye. His peasant women are beautiful, too beautiful, Millet once asserted, to remain in the fields. Critics do not treat his works seriously, although they are very popular. But somehow this subject appeals to the best that is within us. This humble peasant girl, lifted out of the commonplace features of a life of drudgery by the song of a bird, brings to us the thought that even the lowliest may be exalted by the glories of nature, that "June may be had for the asking." And again we read from the poet-painter:

I loved the simple beauty of my native place. . . . Yes, I became one of you, Oh, land where my first joys were felt, and thou didst infuse into my soul the tender beauty of thy carnations, the majesty of the wheat-fields. . . . Oh. land of my childhood, to thee have I given my heart, to thee have I dedicated my life!

7. **Light and Shade.** The position of the sun gives the impression of early dawn merging into the new day.

8. **History.** *The Song of the Lark* was exhibited in the Salon of 1885. It is now in the Henry Field Memorial Collection in the Chicago Art Institute. Signed by Jules Breton. Courrieres, 1884. Size, forty-four inches by thirty-three and one-half inches.

COMMENT

A piece of pure sentimentality; the incident is one that Breton first imagined, and then has worked with the accustomed studio-machinery.—Cook

This year, Breton has as always triumphed at the Exhibition; his peasant girl, haughtily placed, with robust form, is silhouetted upon a sky full of depth. . . . This canvas, of an exquisite sentiment is also full of force in the tones and the values; the pose of the figure is simple and grand without the least playfulness.—M. Ducroz

QUESTIONS

Are you reminded in this picture of another of the artist's subjects? In what respects are they similar? What is the attitude of the girl? In what is she interested? What purpose does the landscape serve? Have you ever walked into the open country at this hour? What were your emotions? Does this girl act naturally at such a time? Do you think it probable that she would pause to listen to a lark's song? Where is the

center of interest? How is it emphasized? Could you suggest
a more pleasing arrangement? In what respects does this
peasant woman differ from those represented by Millet? What
is the expression on her face? What are her pleasing qualities?
What are the most pleasing features in the picture? Does it
appeal to the eye or to the feelings? What definite impression
does the artist seek to give in this subject? Does he give it
plainly? Does the picture reveal any qualities of the artist?
What? In which are you most interested, the young peasant
or the landscape? Why? What is the general impression
given by the landscape? Is it in harmony with the central
thought of the scene?

> Singing thou scalest Heaven upon thy wings,
>   Thou liftest a glad heart into the skies;
> He maketh his own sunrise, while he sings,
>   And turns the dusty Earth to Paradise;
> I see thee sail along
>   Far up the sunny streams,
> Unseen, I hear his song,
>   I see his dreams.
>
> —Frederick Tennyson, *To a Skylark*

THE ARTIST

Breton, *Bre-tôn',* **Jules Adolph Aimé Louis** (1827—1906), a
French artist, was born at Courrieres, Pas du Calais, France.
His artistic gifts were manifest in childhood, and at the age
of sixteen he was sent to Ghent to become the pupil of
de Vigne. In the years that followed he studied with Baron
Wrappirs at Antwerp and with Drolling in Paris. His first
paintings were of historical subjects, but he abandoned this
class of subjects to become a painter of country life. Most of
his paintings of this sort are of scenes in the country of his
boyhood. He rapidly rose to distinction. He was elected to
the Institute in 1886; in 1889 he was awarded the Cross of the
Legion of Honor, and made commander of that organization.

Breton was a writer as well as a painter, and wrote prose
and poetry with equal facility.

He is a skilful, a cultivated and a genuine painter, and has had a history of uninterrupted success.—Stranahan

THE BALLOON

Dupré

For I have learn'd
To look on Nature, not as in the hour
Of thoughtless youth; but hearing oftentimes
The still, sad music of humanity,
. . . And I have felt
A presence that disturbs me with the joy
Of elevated thoughts; a sense sublime
Of something far more deeply interfused,
Whose dwelling is the light of setting suns,
And the round ocean and the living air,
And in the blue sky, and in the mind of man.

—Wordsworth

THE PICTURE

A balloon! See, high above, soaring ever upward to be lost in the clouds, it sails majestically. A group of haymakers in the meadow see it, and pause in their work to follow its course.

What a congenial lot of toilers they seem to be! Very likely they comprise an entire family. Long before sun-up we may be sure they came to this field when the dew yet sparkled on the grass. Here side by side parents and grown sons and daughters have mowed and raked the ripened hay.

The day has been warm, their toil has left the laborers stained and weary. The sultry sun shines full upon the bronzed arms and necks which have been bared for comfort. A broad-rimmed hat shades the face of the father who receives the full glare in his eyes as he watches the balloon. The other man has thrown his hat aside that the summer breeze might fan his brow.

And these women, what loyal, industrious helpers they are. The French peasant woman is not surpassed by any for her resourcefulness and competence in performing the great variety of her tasks. Here to the right the mother, pausing for a moment and shading her eyes, at once receives our respectful attention. We have seen her type in the pictures of other master painters of French working women. We are aware of the multiplicity of her tasks. Her sturdy figure shows no sign of drooping, although the morning hours are well-nigh spent.

How contented they all seem. Does not the element of ownership enter into this toil? Almost as sacred as his faith is the peasant's regard for his independence. Is not prosperity hinted in their comfortable dress, attractive because it is neat, clean and whole? The women wear spotless caps, plain waists, coarse homespun skirts, and clean, comfortably full aprons, while heavy wooden sabots protect their feet from the stubble.

It is the glorious harvest time, when all nature smiles upon the husbandman and bountifully awards his labor. Higher and higher the balloon rises. For a few fleeting moments the workers continue to watch it with breathless interest, while all nature seems hushed as though in sympathy with their uplifted heads and hearts.

> Where the mowers mow the cleanest,
> Where the hay lies thick and greenest,
> There to track the homeward bee,
> That's the way for Billy and me.
>
> But this know, I love to play
> Through the meadow, among the hay;
> Up the water and over the lea,
> That's the way for Billy and me.
>
> —James Hogg

PLAN FOR STUDY

1. **Source of Subject.** A simple country scene in which a balloon is introduced as a motive for a pleasant grouping of a family of harvesters. One critic suggests that the subject was probably evolved during those years when the balloon played an important part in the military operations of the French, in the Franco-Prussian war. It is related that during the siege of Paris, 1870, aeronauts alone kept the unfortunate city in

THE BALLOON.—*Dupré*

touch with the forces in the field. The first balloon ascension took place in France in 1783 and this country, perhaps, leads all others in the development and encouragement of aeronautics. Hence it is easy to see how such a subject might suggest itself to the artist.

2. **Setting.** Here we have a very pleasant bit of open country. The hillside limits the field and contributes a pleasant variety in the lines of the background. The share of canvas occupied by the sky indicates that the motive is here rather than on the land. Note the sunny effect of the picture, the spirit of the season in the new-mown hay and the implements of the workers. Observe the manner of harvesting in the French country districts as compared with our own. The impression of the independence of the laborers is shown in their freedom to pause at will when an occasion like this affords an excuse. There is no suggestion of overseer or other outside authority.

3. **Arrangement.** The chief figures are arranged in the foreground, all intent upon watching the course of the balloon. Each has paused in the several stages of the harvesting, as the various attitudes and positions of the implements indicate. The prevailing lines are horizontal, giving the impression of rest and strength. Observe the pleasant features of the landscape—the hillside, the poplars, the rustic fence and the suggestion of a brook, with the hay in the foreground. Note the impression of dignity, of aspiration, as well as variety in the vertical lines of the trees, the sign of strength in the bared arms of the workers, as well as the effect of the various lines in the figures and the tools. Study the evidences of balance in the arrangement, the one figure of the mower on the left with the group on the right, etc.

The trees are noticeable because of their unusual appearance. Compare the one which reaches to the top of the canvas with those of the middle distance.

4. **Center of Interest.** The balloon is emphasized as the center of interest by the attention of the chief figures and the trend of a number of leading lines. The idea of great distance is conveyed by the position of the balloon. Here the artist with

customary power has given in a very few inches an impression of hundreds of feet.

5. **Supreme Motive.** Dupré was one of the leading painters of the Barbizon group. This explains in part the natural beauty of the landscape in this picture. He painted the open country because he loved it. He was most concerned, however, with the atmospheric effects, especially those which follow or prevail during a storm. He loved to fill his pictures with light and air in which cloud effects might be rendered with surpassing beauty. While he liked best nature in her stormy and magnificent moods, he never tired of painting the simple landscape where just such humble, faithful, industrious labor as this is the chief charm.

6. **Light and Shade.** The lighting is the distinguishing feature of Dupre's paintings, and in this picture we have an example of his best work in that respect. As seen by the shadows, the sun is well up in the sky. It is as if we might see the noon-day lunch follow closely this brief respite during which the laborers watch the balloon. Note the beautiful effects in the soft notes of the far-away hills, the feathery foliage of trees and shrubbery, the bright gleams which thread the hay strewn in the foreground. See how the light seems to penetrate everywhere, and what a warm, sunny quality it gives the scene. Observe the feeling of space between the figures and of the great distance intervening between the several planes of the background. Note the atmospheric qualities as we approach the middle distance, how the outlines of trees become more and more blurred as we go farther back into the composition.

7. **History.** *The Balloon* was painted in 1880 and it now hangs in the Metropolitan Museum of Art, New York City.

QUESTIONS

At what are these people looking? What have they been doing? How do you know? Are they much interested in what they see? How does the artist show this? How many people are there? Do they all stand in the same position? Which seem to be the most interested? Which seem the oldest? The youngest? Of what are they all thinking? How do you know? What time of year is represented in the picture? What time of day? How does the artist show this? What are the most beautiful features of the landscape? Does it seem real to you? Do you think the artist liked to paint such subjects as this one? Why do you think so? Are these people happy? Contented? Industrious? Independent? How does the artist show each of these qualities? What do you think he wishes to tell you in the picture? Does he tell it plainly? Where is the brightest light, the darkest spot? What did you look at first in the picture? What led you to do this? What do you think is the center of interest? What is the title of the picture? Can you suggest a better one? What sounds do these people hear? Do you think their work is pleasant? What are its most pleasant features? Have you ever been in a hayfield? What did you like best to do?

THE HAYMAKERS

Dupré

Labor is health! Lo, the husbandman reaping,
How through his veins goes the life current leaping!
How his strong arm in its stalworth pride sweeping,
True as a sunbeam the swift sickle glides.

—Frances S. Osgood

The sunburnt mowers are in the swath—
Swing, swing, swing!
The towering lilies loath
Tremble and totter and fall;
The meadow-rue
Dashes its tassels of golden dew;
And the keen blade sweeps
O'er all—
Swing, swing, swing!

—Myron B. Benton

THE PICTURE

What rollicking, carefree words are in this song of the mowers. Do not these two men seem to be swinging along with hearts atune to its merry sentiment? High up in a cloudless sky the sun that ripens the hay smiles down upon them. On every hand, as far as eye can see, the brown and gold of grass and grain sway joyfully to every breeze that stirs. Birds sing, bright field-flowers toss their heads gleefully, while the fragrance of the new-mown hay fills the summer air.

See, this strong man, who has been mowing since earliest dawn, is swinging the scythe without a trace of weariness. For a moment only, his companion has straightened up to sharpen his blade.

Behind him, where the scythes have laid the hay in even rows, another worker is eating her noon-day lunch. Her's is a well-earned rest from the wearisome task of raking. See, there in the smooth, even mound beyond is evidence of her faithful toil. These sinewy arms that move the scythe are not more tireless and active than her own. Years of manifold tasks, both of the home and field, have fitted her for the unending cycle of farm labor of which this scene represents but a single phase. We see her resting now. Unconcerned with the labor about her, unmindful of the long, weary hours that still lie before her, she gives herself up wholly to the few moments of this lunching period.

At her side a covered basket protects the lunch for the men from the dust and heat of the hayfield. Her capable hands have prepared plain, wholesome food for them as well as for herself. She wears the customary cap of the French working woman. A plain but durable dress and heavy sabots make up her work-a-day attire. In the distance a hayrick or two and a clump of trees suggest a hamlet of homes, while beyond, the field stretches for miles and miles to meet the sky.

What comfortable workers they all seem to be. True enough, the pieced-out blouses and patched trousers speak of poverty —but it is poverty of the respectable sort. The patches are neatly done, the trousers and blouses are clean and whole. There is not the faintest suggestion of thriftlessness in dress or action. A sense of proprietorship is suggested in the proud, energetic bearing of the men. These few acres belong to them.

This worker who soberly braces the handle of his heavy implement while he gives the blade a sharper edge is absorbed in his task. His toil is of the most serious sort. The successful gathering of this harvest is of the utmost importance. Clear skies today may be followed by stormy ones tomorrow. Hungry little mouths in the home for which he works will depend throughout the winter upon what he is able to reap at such a time as this.

We cannot see the features very well, but there is a suggestion of strength, of grim resolve in the rugged contour of each bronzed face. Before them stretches the hayfield in brown, waving billows. Behind them, their sturdy strokes have left prostrate in the sunshine swaths of mown grass, fragrant and

THE HAYMAKERS.—*Dupré*

flower bedecked. Their labor is of the most wearisome sort, and only arms with muscles hardened by years of just such labor as this can swing these heavy blades with such ease, grace and rhythm.

> July is just in the nick of time!
> (Hay-weather, hay-weather;)
> The mid-summer month is the golden prime
> For haycocks smelling of clover and thyme;—
> (Swing all together!)
> July is just in the nick of time!
>
> Still hiss the scythes!
> Shudder the grasses' defenceless blades—
> The lily-throng writhes;
> The mowers, each a step in advance of his fellow,
> Time their stroke with a glance
> Of swerveless force;
> And far through the meadow leads their course—
> Swing, swing, swing!

—The Mowers

PLAN FOR STUDY

1. Source of Subject. Undoubtedly this simple scene of rustic labor was the result of many studies in the fields of L'Isle Adam, where Dupré settled in 1849.

2. Setting. The setting is a simple haymaking scene in France. The predominating horizontal lines convey a general impression of repose, and the high horizon suggests that the motive of the subject is in a great field. In the background we see the dim outlines of the homes of the laborers.

Observe in the peasant costume the blouses and broad-brimmed hats of the men, and the cap of the woman. Coarse and patched these costumes may be, but in the dress of each figure we see a suggestion of respectability. Everything in the picture combines to produce a typical rural scene in France.

3. Arrangement. The three workers are arranged in a line along the swath of hay. In advance is the sturdy form of one mower in action, behind him the other has straightened up to sharpen his blade, while a few steps back the sole woman of the scene, who has been raking, is seated taking some sort of refreshment. Behind, stretches the field to meet the sky, which occupies a comparatively small part of the canvas. Note the variety of lines in the action of the chief figures, how the strong impression of movement is given by the repetition of the slanting lines.

Observe the play of muscle in the strong forearm of the first mower, and how the weight of the body is carried by the right forward leg and the ball of the left foot. The action is easy and natural and shows close study on the part of the artist. Note the play of wrinkles in his blouse as he bends to his task; also the attitude of the man who braces his implement as he sharpens the blade. Is there not an impression of its weight in the way he balances it? Study the representation of the several planes of the composition. The bare suggestive qualities of the trees and hayricks in the background compared with the detail in the grass and flowers in the immediate foreground. Observe the variety in the postures of the workers, how unity is effected by their arrangement. Would this have been possible had the woman been represented in action?

4. **Center of Interest.** Observe that the blades in both instances, the one about to cut the stalks, the other being sharpened, seem the ultimate direction toward which the lines of the composition all trend. While the chief figures hold a large share of our interest, we are at first concerned with the blades. This center of interest is further emphasized by the brightest light on the lower blade and the strongest dark on the upper one.

5. **Supreme Motive.** It would seem that the artist's supreme motive was to set forth the sturdy character and worth of the French peasantry. This is a landscape represented by one who loved to paint it. While it marks a departure from his usual treatment, for Dupré loved the tragic element in nature—the gale, the storm clouds, the bitter blasts—he could at all times with deep enjoyment paint in convincing manner such simple rustic scenes of farm labor as this. While not himself bowed down by the drudgery, the serious aspect of the peasant's existence, as was Millet, he was nevertheless a careful student

in the fields of L'Isle Adam, where he watched the various phases of toil in the open country. From nature alone he received his inspiration and we may be sure he represented the workers so closely associated with her, with only sympathy for their hard lot. Note the sturdy, sober, thrifty aspect of these men. Are they not true men of the fields—men of character and worth?

6. **Light and Shade**. Dupré was a master in representing light and air in his pictures, and this quality is well brought out in *The Haymakers*. The charm and beauty of the subject are almost entirely dependent upon the light and shade effects.

Determine from the shadows the direction from which the light comes, and observe how, in the sunny glow, all parts of the landscape are softened and held together; also how the suggestion of movement is conveyed in the changing lights and shadows on the hay. Nature is never at rest, and we who have walked in a meadow on a summer day can appreciate the fleeting shadows, the windswept grass and foliage which the artist here so effectively renders.

7. **History**. *The Haymakers* was painted in 1880.

COMMENT

Essentially a man of peace, he (Dupré) did not indeed, introduce fresh life into the art world when he led the way into pasture lands, farms, and fields, the quiet forest or the peasant hut; but his compositions are always quiet and pastoral pictures of the peace of a country life.—Mollett

In him are heard the mighty fugues of Romanticism. The trees live, the waves laugh and weep, the sky sings and wails, and the sun, like a great conductor, determines the harmony of the concert.—Muther

Delighted in the play of the clouds in the heavens, so that his land is often but a necessary complement of the composition.—Von Mach

QUESTIONS

What is this picture about? What are these men doing? This woman? Are they all doing the same thing? Have you ever seen men doing this kind of work? Did they use the same tools as these men are using? Where did this farming

scene take place? What has the woman been doing? Is she
tired? What time of day is it? What season of the year?
Of what are these men thinking? What is the expression on
their faces? Do they seem happy? Proud? Contented? Do
they seem to enjoy their work? What makes you think so?
How much work have they done? Do they move along very
fast? Are these men strong? Capable? How does the artist
tell this? How are these workers dressed? Why do they
wear these wooden shoes? Are their scythes heavy? What
makes you think so? What colors would you use in coloring
this picture? What sounds do you seem to hear? What
actions do you seem to see? In which are you most interested,
the workers or the landscape? Why?

THE ARTIST

Dupré, *Dü-prā'*, **Jules** (1812—1889), a French painter, was
born at Nantes, France. He began his career as a painter of
porcelain in his father's pottery works. In 1831 he began an
art course in Paris. He studied under Langier and Pils, and
was influenced by Hobema, Ruysdael and Constable. He was
one of the chief members of the Barbizon group of artists, and
was associated with Corot, Diaz, Troyon and Millet. He was
honored at three different times with the medal of the Exposition Universelle. He had studios in the forest of Fontainebleau
and L'Isle Adam, where he died. He was one of the most
noted landscape painters of his time.

Light is the charm of his picture.—Von Mach

Dupré is always a great, true, convincing poet.—Muther

The landscape in this picture is agreeably painted . . . shows Julien
Dupré in a softer mood.—Cook

He is always true in his rendering of the atmosphere, of the cooling
moisture in it that rises from the saturated vegetation after a storm . . .
or the dance of a sunbeam, or drift of a cloud, or the mirror of the sky
in a pool; it is always the air, real air, that you seem to breathe, that
fascinates you and gives life and reality to the canvas.—Meyer

AT THE WATERING TROUGH

Dagnan-Bouveret

A country life is sweet!
In moderate cold and heat,
To walk in the air how pleasant and fair!
In every field of wheat,
The fairest of flowers adorning the bowers,
And every meadow's brow;
So that I say, no courtier may
Compare with them who clothe in gray,
And follow the useful plow.

—Anonymous

THE PICTURE

The day's work is done. Tired and thirsty after the long hours of steady pulling in the furrows, these horses with their driver have returned to the barn. Here at the trough with its clear, cool water they stand. Close by, their master, pipe in hand, his whip dangling from his right arm, holds the reins as he waits patiently for them to drink their fill. One, a powerful black fellow, has already lifted his head and meditates contentedly. The other still drinks with evident enjoyment. To the right of the man we have a glimpse of the distant field. Such are the commonplace details of this subject, a scene such as we might come upon in any country place. Yet what interest there is in its portrayal.

The most satisfying time of the day has arrived. The hot, weary hours of strain and pull are gone. In store for these horses there is a generous reward of grain and hay. This kind-hearted, thoroughly capable farmer has never failed them.

Erect and independent in bearing, he is a true representative of that proud, contented class, the French landowners. Even in his work-a-day garb there is a suggestion of pride and attention to personal appearance. The broad hat shades a

AT THE WATERING TROUGH.—*Dagnan Bouveret*

bronzed face, attractive for its frank expression. The blouse with its collar unbuttoned and sleeves rolled back is clean and whole. Neat fitting trousers tucked below the knees into leather boots give a most comfortable aspect to the man, quite different from that of the general type of French peasant. There is something convincing about this sturdy figure. His is a vitality and heartiness that only a life in the open country can give. Then, too, he comes of a sturdy race who for generations past have plowed and sowed and reaped in this field where today he proudly claims title.

> Happy the man whose work and care
> A few paternal acres bound,
> Content to breathe his native air
> In his own ground.

—Pope

But if we are interested in the owner, what shall we say of these faithful horses which make his prosperity possible? Surely theirs is no small contribution. Without them how could acres and acres of ground be turned and prepared for the seed? Upon the intelligent use of their strength depends in large measure the labors of the field.

PLAN FOR STUDY

1. **Source of Subject.** The artist conceived this subject while visiting one summer at the country place of his father-in-law. A bit of interesting history is given in connection with it. The artist, whose aim it was to be exact in representing what he painted, of necessity contrived several devices for painting this group directly from nature. One device consisted in making a plaster cast of the horses' backs by laying over them cloths soaked in plaster of paris. When sufficiently hardened, the harness was set on them, the makeshift proving a satisfactory substitution for the real models.

2. **Setting.** Here is portrayed a very common scene in country life. The farmer and his team have returned home at the end of their day's work. The field from which they came is dimly seen in the background. Compare the harness with that in our country. How does it differ? The meditative

expression of the man and one horse and the slow, satisfied drinking of the other convey an impression of quiet and repose.

3. **Arrangement.** The chief figures are arranged in the immediate foreground, the white horse with head lowered serving to balance the figure of the man. It will be observed that this is essentially a figure picture. There is a suggestion of the triangular in the upper portion. Observe especially the sympathetic study revealed in the attitudes of the horses. The white horse while drinking makes little ripples in the water as he moves his nose about. Note the characteristic expression of the eyes of the animals. So natural and suggestive are their positions that we would not be surprised to see them make a number of those movements so characteristic of horses drinking.

4. **Center of Interest.** Where does your eye rest longest in the scene? What does this tell you about the center of interest?

5. **Supreme Motive.** Dagnan was a close student of nature. His distinguishing characteristic was the sympathetic and accurate treatment of his subjects. No painter was moved by a higher motive to paint truthfully and sincerely. Like many other painters of rustic scenes, he never tired of painting the commonplace features of country life. What in this simple scene "ennobles the commonplace?" We would say, above all, character. For like all truly great artists, Dagnan recognized character in humble folk as well as in those more highly gifted and intellectual. Can we be mistaken in the character of these noble horses, so patient and faithful in their service for man? Is not this honest and hearty man a type of those to whom the world looks for its sustenance?

> These are the hands whose steady labor brings
> The peasant's food, the golden pomp of kings.

6. **Light and Shade.** The lighting is pleasing. The shadows of the figures are indistinct, hence the disagreement on the part of some as to the time of day here represented. What is your opinion? The highest light is on the head of the white horse and the corner of the trough. Note how the light brings out the details of the harness, revealing the painstaking care with which the artist painted it. Was this necessary? Would

we have been as much pleased with a broader treatment?
Observe how the light brings out clearly the features of the
man against the black rim of his hat, also the rendering of the
horses' coats. Is texture here well brought out? Of what
material is the watering trough?

7. **History**. This picture was painted in 1885, and it now
hangs in the Luxembourg Gallery, Paris.

QUESTIONS

What do you see in this picture? What have the horses been
doing? Are they tired? Which seems more weary? How
has the artist shown this? At what is this man looking? Does
he seem tired? Of what is he thinking? Is he proud? Contented? What does he hold in his hand? Where does he carry
his whip? Do you imagine him to be a kind master? Do his
horses seem fond of him? How is he dressed? What are the
most pleasing things about him? Where have they been working? What is the expression in the horses' eyes? Is the
expression the same in both horses? Is the action of the white
horse natural? What actions do you seem to see? What
sounds do you seem to hear? What time of day do you think
it is? How do these horses serve this man? What does he do
for them in return for their services? Do they seem well
cared for?

> What though our burden be not light,
>   We need not toil from morn to night;
> The respite of the mid-day hour
>   Is in the thankful creature's power.
>
> Each field is then a hallowed spot,
>   An altar is each man's cot
> A church in every grove that spreads
>   Its living roof above our heads.
>
> Help with thy grace, through life's short day,
>   Our upward and our downward way;
> And glorify for us the west,
>   When we shall sink to final rest.
>
> —Holmes, *The Plowman*

THE ARTIST

Dagnan-Bouveret, *Dän-yon′* *Böv-rā′,* **Adolphe Jean** (1852—), a French painter, was born in Paris. His father was a merchant and lived in Brazil, but the artist spent his childhood with his grandfather in France, where he was educated. He was a pupil of Gerome and a member of the Ecole des Beaux Arts. His first picture, *A Wedding at the Photographer's,* was exhibited at the Salon of 1870. In 1885 he received the award of the Legion of Honor, and in 1892 was made an officer of that organization. In 1899 he received his first medal at the Salon, it being awarded for his *Breton Women at the Pardon.* His most noted pictures are *Madonna,* at Munich, and *Madonna-of-the-Workshop* in the Metropolitan Museum.

A man of the most sympathetic nature, and the kindest heart.
It appears to Dagnan, quality is greater than sincerity.

Dagnan is at once a poet and a great artist.—Karageorgevitch

In the *Horses at the Watering Trough* . . . at the Luxembourg Gallery . . . and other works, I have seen enough to convince me that Dagnan-Bouveret is one of the ablest painters of our times.—Coffin

RETURN TO THE FARM

Troyon

Shepherds all and maidens fair,
Fold your flocks up; for the air
Begins to thicken, and the sun
Already his great course hath run.
See the dewdrops, how they kiss
Every little flower that is;
Hanging on their velvet heads,
Like a string of crystal beads.

  —Beaumont and Fletcher, *Folding the Flocks*

THE PICTURE

Night is coming on. Out in the quiet meadow the cattle and sheep, after the long hours of peaceful feeding, instinctively turn toward home. The good herdsman throws down the bars, the sheep-dog rounds up every member of the flock, and the tramp of hoofs is heard along the lane. Here, where the road turns, they are coming toward us out of the deep shadow of a clump of trees.

A little black and white collie barking excitedly as he chases back and forth across the path leads the way. Close behind, two patient cows follow slowly and sedately. At the right a flock of sheep patter leisurely along. A single donkey, somewhat apart from the others, brings up the rear. In a nearby pool a couple of cows are standing knee deep, taking a last cooling draught. Still others are grazing along the grassy slope.

On they come. In a few moments we may expect them to round the bend in the road and be lost to sight. The alert dog will not suffer them to stray far, we may be sure. He is the protector of the flock. His is the safe leadership that comes from an entire life of service and training for this very work. Can we wonder that he is so proudly active in his care of them? These gentle sheep that take no apparent notice of him do not

RETURN TO THE FARM.—*Troyon*

know that he is of the type that will risk life for their safety. The good herdsman knows it though, and loves his dog as only an appreciative master can.

How truthfully the cows are portrayed in their various attitudes as they pass along. It is the most natural thing in the world for some to loiter in the tempting green spots along the roadside, and for others to wade out into such a delightful pool. Then is not the action of this one on the left, vigorously reaching back her head to chase away some troublesome insect, perfectly natural?

The donkey seems out of place and a trifle lonely in a company with tastes so widely divergent from his own. His ears, donkey-like, are lifted to catch every sound. Especially is he concerned with the actions of the dog.

Lower and lower the sun is sinking. Soon it will drop behind the western rim. The evening winds stir the foliage of the trees, and sweep into silvery wavelets the surface of the pool. The clouds rolling up in the gorgeous depths of the sky take on a softer glow as the shadows lengthen in the lane far below. Only the barking of the dog and the patter of hoofs break the dreamy silence in which the landscape salutes the close of day.

> From upland slopes I see the cows file by
> Lowing, great-chested, down the homeward trail,
> By dusking fields and meadows shining pale
> With moon-tipped dandelions.
>
> —Archibald Lampman

PLAN FOR STUDY

1. **Source of Subject.** A group of animals returning to the farm forms the center of interest in this charming landscape. In this simple scene of the open country Troyon has touched with warmest colors the most commonplace material. Such a time of day when over the landscape there is spread the enchantment of a summer evening, he likes best to represent. We who have wandered along a country road at the sunset hour can truly appreciate the motive of this subject. Is there not an inexplicable something, a strong emotional appeal, to

say the least, at that period of the day when the summer sunshine merges into the evening glow?

> The curfew tolls the knell of parting day,
> The lowing herd wind slowly o'er the lea,
> The plowman homeward plods his weary way,
> And leaves the world to darkness and to me.
>
> Now fades the glimmering landscape on the sight,
> And all the air a solemn stillness holds,
> Save where the beetle wheels his droning flight,
> And drowsy tinklings lull the distant folds.
>
> —Thomas Gray

Troyon was first of all a painter of cattle. In his representation of them he was unexcelled, if not unequalled. No less able was he in portraying sheep. He always represented them in a landscape which had a distinctive charm and appeal of its own. With poetic insight he observed the variable moods of nature and, better than all, he so related his animals to their natural setting that we "can no more separate the cows from the landscape than we can the sense from the melody in a verse of Tennyson."

2. **Setting.** The dominant note is found in the effect of the evening hour on the landscape, apart from the action of the animals which give life to the scene. Then, too, even the animals instinctively respond to it, for do they not contentedly turn their steps homeward? Note the characteristic Troyon sky, deep and filled with rapidly changing storm clouds. Does not this feature add to the power and sublimity of the scene?

Observe the effect of several pleasing features of the setting —the pool, the wide sunny lane, the distant reaches of field on either side of the clump of trees in the background. Note the activity of the dog—the suggestion that it gives of the homeward direction of the flock. Observe the impression of repose, and discover how it is secured. What besides the low, flat lines, the soft misty contours of the foliage, contribute to this impression?

3. **Arrangement.** The pleasing arrangement adds much to the interest of the subject. First, observe that the general direction of the animals is toward us, but note how skilfully

the artist has avoided a monotony in grouping. It is as if he paid special attention, with much preliminary study, to individual animal traits. Two cows, exhibiting in their slow and quiet progress all the essential characteristics of their breed, are arranged in the central foreground, their strong bodies relieved against the shadowy foliage in the background. The dog dashes back and forth across the immediate foreground, while to the left and well in the lead, the flock of sheep are painted with evident attention to their matted fleeces. Note how almost every possible position is invented to show the different characteristics and qualities of the animals. In the low horizon line we see the pleasing variety given by the rounded tops of the trees to the general low and flat lines of the composition.

Observe how balance is secured with an avoidance of equal spacing. For example, the largest clump of trees at the turn of the lane is placed well to the right in the middle distance, and is balanced by a smaller clump to the left. Notice how the impression of amplitude is given; also the treatment of the trees in the different planes, and the impression of great distances between them. The outlines are softened with varying degrees through the atmosphere.

4. **Center of Interest.** We are not quite sure that Troyon ever intended that his landscape should be subordinated to the animals with which he added life and action to it. We would say that the motive for this subject, however, is to be found in the landscape and that the animals are but a part of the general scheme to emphasize the dominant note—its tranquil aspect. Nevertheless, our interest centers first upon the two foremost cows which mark the highest light of the picture and then moves rapidly to the lesser details which go to make up the whole. Observe how unity is secured, even though there is a wide variance in the attitude and position of the animals.

5. **Light and Shade.** The lighting is a most pleasing feature. The long shadows tell us that the sun is low in the sky and that the light comes from the right. The effect of the cloudy sky is to afford a magnificent spectacle as it is glorified by the evening light, as well as to give the impression of power and

force in the landscape. Note how the high light brings out the contours of the sheep, the cream and reddish brown of the hides of the cows, and the curly hair of the dog which marks the darkest place in the scene. The approach of twilight seems strongest in the trees of the middle distance, and there is an impression of movement in the blurred outlines—can you picture the ever changing spectacle of the sky?

6. **History.** *The Return to the Farm* was first exhibited in 1859, and again in 1865. After Troyon's death, it was presented by his mother to the French nation. It now hangs in the Louvre Gallery, Paris. A similar subject, *The Return of the Flock*, was sold in 1906 for $42,250 at the Joseph Jefferson sale. Another *Return to the Farm* by Troyon brought $65,000 at the Henry sale recently.

COMMENT

His sheep are rendered with palpable, bleating truth.—Blanc

However excellent may be Troyon's cattle or horses, they are, in all his greater works subordinate to the scheme of landscape which constitutes the picture.—Thomson

Troyon's cattle pieces are pastoral poems—as true to nature and character of the artist's country as those of Van de Velde, Paul Potter or the Mauve of our own days are to their native Holland.—Cook

QUESTIONS

How many different animals do you see in this picture? Where are they going? Where have they been? Where is the herdsman? What is he supposed to do for them? Does he have an assistant? Whom? What is the dog doing? Is he a good protector of the flock? How do you know? How many sheep do you see? Are they all equally distinct? Why not? Is this true to nature? What do they give the farmer in return for his care of them? Are they alarmed? Obedient? Are they always so? How many cows do you see? Do you see all of them quite plainly? Why not? Is this true to nature? What are the cows doing? Are they all doing the same thing? Is it more pleasing that they should all be moving together? Why? Do you see the donkey? What time of day is it? What season of the year? How does the artist show this? What are the most charming features of the landscape? What are its chief points of beauty? What do you like best about it? In which are you most interested, the animals or the landscape? Why? What seems to be the spirit of the landscape? Of the animals? What colors would you use in coloring this scene? What sounds do you seem to hear? What natural actions do you seem to see in the animals? Do you think the painter loved the open country? Does this picture appeal to the eye or to the feeling? What feeling does it give you?

> And what is so rare as a day in June?
>   Then, if ever, come perfect days;
> Then Heaven tries the earth if it be in tune,
>   And over it softly her warm ear lays;
> Whether we look, or whether we listen,
>   We hear life murmur, or see it glisten;
> Every clod feels a stir of might,
>   An instinct within it that reaches and towers,
> And, groping blindly above it for light,
>   Climbs to a soul in grass and flowers.
>   —Lowell, *The Vision of Sir Launfal*

THE ARTIST

Troyon, *Trwä-yôn',* **Constant** (1810—1865), a landscape and animal painter, was born at Sevres, France. His father was connected with a famous pottery manufactory, and Troyon began his career as a decorator of pottery. Later he was a pupil of Riocruix and Paupart. At the age of twenty-one he began to paint landscapes. Later he visited Holland and studied in the Dutch School, giving special attention to the works of Paul Potter and Cuyp. As a result of this study he became an animal painter of the first rank. He was awarded first-class medals in 1846, 1852 and 1855, and received the Decoration of the Legion of Honor in 1849. All his famous pictures were painted between 1850 and 1864. He died in Paris in 1865.

Troyon's genius is not to be questioned; he is the first of modern animal painters and resembles no other.—Cook

THE WINDMILL

Ruysdael

Behold! a giant am I!
  Aloft here in my tower,
  With my granite jaws I devour
The maize, and the wheat, and the rye,
  And grind them into flour.

I look down over the farms;
  In the fields of grain I see
  The harvest that is to be,
And I fling to the air my arms, ·
  For I know it is all for me.

. . . . .

I stand here in my place,
  With my foot on the rock below,
  And whichever way it may blow,
I meet it face to face
  As a brave man meets his foe.

And while we wrestle and strive,
  My master, the miller, stands
  And feeds me with his hands:
For he knows who makes him thrive,
  Who makes him lord of lands.

—Longfellow, *The Windmill*

THE PICTURE

Let us enter at once into the spirit of this old windmill. How like a lonely sentinel it stands at the riverside and reaches high up against the clouds of an evening sky. Motionless in the ominous calm which precedes the gale, its great arms await the first breath of wind which will start them on their lofty whirl.

At a glance we note the lesser objects of the scene. Here

101

at the foot of the hill, the broad winding river reflects the glories of the sky. In the distance a boat, its sails flat and still, drifts lazily with the current. Through the gathering gloom the steeples and roofs bring a suggestion of a quaint Dutch village, while in the path along the riverside some of its inhabitants are returning from their day's work in the fields.

How the approaching twilight throws its somber, magic spell about the mill. Built solidly and well to stand the stress of warring elements, it has stood for centuries with its enormous arms outstretched to capture the winds.

With the sincere feeling that such an hour and scene inspires, let us in fancy climb the winding stairway to the balcony. Here we are impressed with a feeling of our own insignificance as we look far out over the reaches of earth and sky. A spirit of foreboding, of melancholy prevails. All nature sings an evening song in a minor key. It is as though the trees and man-made structures were saddened by the influence of an approaching storm. A mysterious aspect of nature, too, is echoed in the silent river which, broad and majestic, sweeps out of our sight past the curve of the distant hill. From what hillside did it spring, what woods, what fields of growing crops, what haunts of men has it passed on its journey to the sea?

What power and majesty in the sky. What hidden force is impending in the clouds which almost obscure it? We glance upward along the weatherbeaten sides of the tower, and a new conception of man's place in the universe comes to us. Marvelous is his power over the natural elements when he studies them in conformity with the divine plan. These great arms impede the unseen winds and compel them to turn the machinery of the mill. Man fashions sails that force the winds to move the cargoes of the great ocean commerce. He constructs dams over which the water of streams is lifted to turn the wheels that grind the grain or propel the looms. Over the sea, too, he has shown dominion. By his own efforts he reared the dykes to wrest from the waves these acres of land that give sustenance to a nation.

THE WINDMILL.—*Ruysdael*

Lower and lower the evening shadows close in about the scene. Up from the west the storm clouds continue to roll and overcast the mellow glow of the sky. Full upon the gray walls of the mill the sinking sun sheds a soft lustre. No breeze yet ruffles the surface of the stream, but the lull is only momentary. Even as we look we may expect to see the great arms of the tower begin to revolve like the wings of some monstrous bird. In the distance the men in the boats await anxiously the gust that will fill their sails. Silently we pause for a moment with these three women on the hillside in a parting look upon the scene. As they turn once more to the village, we too retrace our steps and leave the old mill to wrestle alone with the storm.

> Suddenly all the sky is hid,
> As with the shutting of a lid,
> One by one great drops are falling
>   Doubtful and slow,
> Down the pane they are crookedly crawling,
>   And the wind breathes low;
> Slowly the circles widen on the river,
>   Widen and mingle, one and all;
> Here and there the slender flowers shiver,
>   Struck by an icy rain-drop's fall.
> Now on the hills I hear the thunder mutter,
>   The wind is gathering in the west.
> The upturned leaves first whiten and flutter,
>   Then droop to a fitful rest.
> Up from the stream with sluggish flap
>   Struggles the gull and floats away;
> Nearer and nearer rolls the thunder clap,
>   We shall not see the sun go down today:
> Now leaps the wind on the sleepy marsh,
>   And tramples the grass with terrified feet.
> The startled river turns leaden and harsh.
>   You can hear the quick heart of the terrified tempest beat.

> —Lowell, *A Summer Storm*

PLAN FOR STUDY

1. Source of Subject. The scene of this picture is from the immediate vicinity of the Dutch village of Wyk-by-Duurstede on the Rhine river a few miles from Utrecht, Holland. We can imagine the special appeal such a subject made to one who was only concerned with recording upon his canvas the impression that a natural scene made upon him.

2. **Setting.** A typical Dutch landscape—flat without variety, and with a body of water and a characteristic windmill. The suggestion of the nearby village in the steeples and roofs and the solid effect of the structures impart an impression of strength to the scene. Note the effect of the leading flat lines relieved only by the dominant vertical of the windmill, the masts of the vessels, the spires, the figures of the women and the piling in the breakwater.

Observe the space occupied by the sky—two-thirds of the canvas—and the impression of solemnity and power it gives. Note, too, the presence of the wee human figures in the infinite stretch of earth and sky, how they emphasize the vastness of the scene. Observe also the suggestion of the man on the balcony in connection with the last thought. Note the impression made by the broad, silent river and the effect of the rounding the curve in the distance. Does not this add a touch of mystery to its silent flow? Are we not inclined to think of its source and the scenes through which it has come? In the fast gathering clouds is a suggestion of a coming storm quite in accord with the prevailing melancholy aspect. We feel the impression of tremendous force of the elements contrasted with the momentary lull. The unruffled surface of the river; the sails flat and still, and the motionless arms of the windmill, all show that not a breath of wind is stirring. What does the time of day add to the general impression?

3. **Arrangement.** The composition is remarkably simple. Observe the small number of details and with what ease the mind grasps them at once, even as we instantly center our interest upon the strongest feature—the mill. It is not the business of the landscape painter to record accurately the scene before him. If this were true the charm of many a landscape picture would be utterly lost. A truly great painter of nature has an instinctive power of selection. He seeks and finds in commonplace scenes hidden beauty which the ordinary eye would not discern. In the spirit of his own nature he studies the scene and records his own impression of it for

our enjoyment. If he loves the landscape, if his technique is faultless, if his soul is pure, and his motive lofty, his painting, however commonplace the scene may be, becomes a really great work of art.

Here the painter chose to make the windmill the dominant impression. Place a piece of paper over it and observe how uninteresting, flat and spiritless the landscape becomes. How completely the mass of details have been subordinated to the center of interest. Look where we will in the scene and the mill is constantly in our vision; the tower—its great bulk, strong, impressive and full of suggestion, of aspiration, dignity and power—serves to connect the land and the sky. No single feature in the picture is strong enough to hold our undivided interest. Observe the principle of perspective in representing the different planes, also the great distances on land and the limitless character of the vast dome of the heavens. Note the impression of space and how this is effected by the low horizon line; also the variety of lines that serve to break the flat character of the landscape. What suggestion relative to motion do you find in the position of the arms of the mill? Is this arrangement the most effective? Point out examples of balance in the composition.

4. **Center of Interest.** Show in as many ways as you can why the mill is the strongest object and therefore the center of interest. Is this picture a good example of unity in a painting? Explain.

5. **Supreme Motive.** Ruysdael was a melancholy spirit. He had much to make him so. His life was one long struggle with poverty, in which there came no adequate recognition of his power as a landscape painter. In his last years he was the recipient of charity, and death found him in the almshouse of his native town. Naturally his temperament was a sober, thoughtful and even gloomy one. Naturally, too, it colored to a large degree his representation of every landscape subject. In fact, his work has been criticised because it is never lifted from the serious, melancholy vein. When we remember that true art is largely subjective, that is to say, when it gives us the impression which the natural scene made upon the mind

of the painter, or, still better, when we look at nature through the eyes of the artist, we recognize at once the character of the man revealed in this landscape with the mill. If we had no biography of Ruysdael this picture would suffice to give us very truthfully the dominant qualities of the man. Just what motive prompted him in painting this subject? Might he not have answered—

Pray for my soul. More things are wrought by prayer
Than this world dreams of. Wherefore, let thy voice
Rise like a fountain for me night and day.
For what are men better than sheep or goats
That nourish a blind life within the brain,
If, knowing God, they lift not hands of prayer
Both for themselves and those who call them friends?
For so the whole round earth is every way
Bound by gold chains about the feet of God. —*Tennyson.*

6. **Light and Shade.** It was a peculiar quality of Ruysdael that he never used the real sun. In this scene, he brings the gleams from a sinking sun to light up his beautiful cloud effects, as well as to diffuse a mellow glow upon the water and the gray wall. Note the touch of the mysterious and solemn in the shadowy portions; the soft effect where the light merges into the dark, and the effect of the shadowy land masses brought up against the high light of the distant horizon.

8. **History.** Painted on canvas, and measuring two feet eight inches high by three feet three inches wide, this picture was bequeathed to the Ryks Museum, Amsterdam, Holland, 1854 (A. Vander Hoop collection). "A better name for it would be *The Windmill.* Under this title no one could without disadvantage treat a subject which found in Ruysdael's hands its incomparable, its typical expression."

The mill stands at this spot where the Rhine divides to form the Lek and Kromme Rhyn (or "Crooked Rhine"). Houses now stand where the low trees are seen round the mill. It is not so high as it seems in the picture, and the lower part is now square and not round, and has a passage through it.—De Groot

COMMENT

One of Ruysdael's greatest and most celebrated works—a veritable masterpiece.—Masters in Art

It ought to be seen to learn, from a master who never feared to degrade himself because he was not a man to stoop, how a subject can be elevated when a man is himself a lofty spirit—to learn that there is nothing ugly for an eye which sees beauty, no littleness for a great sensitiveness—to learn, in a word, what the art of painting becomes when practiced by a noble mind.—Fromentin

QUESTIONS

Of what is this a picture? What feeling do you have as you look upon this scene? Where does your eye first rest? In what are you most interested? What is the strongest object in the picture? What are the people doing? Can you see them plainly? Are you much interested in them? Where do you suppose these women are going? What have they been doing? What are the men in the boat doing? What is the condition of the weather? What makes you feel that a storm is coming up? What are the never failing signs? From what country is this scene taken? What helped you to recognize this? What time of day is it? What season of the year? How does the painter show this? What is the general direction of the leading lines? Is there any variety? Where? What is the impression given by the horizontal lines? The vertical? Which of these are the stronger in the picture? How much of the space does the sky occupy? What does this tell you about the artist's motive? What impression does the deep sky add to the scene? From what direction does the light come? Where is the highest light? The shadow? What do you suppose the artist is trying to tell us in this picture? Does it inspire you with a cheerful feeling or a solemn, sad one? What traits of character of the painter does the subject reveal? What are the chief points of beauty in the landscape? Why are you especially interested in the old mill? Have you ever seen any other picture of a Dutch landscape? In what respects was it similar to this one?

THE ARTIST

Ruysdael, *Rois'däl,* **Jacob** (about 1625—1682), one of the greatest of Dutch landscape painters, was born at Haarlem, Netherlands. He studied under his uncle, Solomon Ruysdael, and was admitted to membership in the Guild of Painters in Haarlem in 1648. Notwithstanding his great ability, his life was one of long struggle with poverty, and he died in an almshouse in his native town. His industry was remarkable, more than 450 of his paintings having been catalogued. He is represented in many of the leading art galleries in Europe.

In truth, Ruysdael's art consists of that combination of truth to nature and of imagination which has made him the greatest landscape-painter of Holland, and has caused his pictures to rank, at all times, among the most admired treasures of art.—De Groot

THE HORSE FAIR

Bonheur

Gamarra is a dainty steed,
Strong, black, and of a noble breed,
Full of fire, and full of bone,
With all his line of fathers known;
Fine his nose, his nostrils thin,
But blown abroad by the pride within!
His mane is like a river flowing,
And his eyes like embers glowing
In the darkness of the night,
And his pace as swift as light.

—''Barry Cornwall,'' *The Blood Horse*

THE PICTURE

Prancing, rearing, plunging, and grandly curveting, a host of the finest horses of Paris, with strong necks arching and manes flowing, sweep past with majestic pace, rapid, sure, triumphant.

Proudly conscious of our admiration, composed and dignified in the face of it, they are crowding with hilarious spirits to the market place. Did ever kings of the grandest courts of old in their jeweled robes impress their humble subjects with such majesty and power as this? Did Caesar, lordly emperor of the whole world, move with such conscious dignity beneath the triumphal arches of his own beloved city? Before the kingly grace of these noble steeds we humbly bow.

Could a more suitable highway be found for such a royal procession? Down an avenue bright with sunshine and fringed with beautiful trees, the horses are prancing gayly to the exhibition.

Steed threatens steed, in high and boastful neighs,
Piercing the night's dull ear.

110

THE HORSE FAIR.—*Bonheur*

Pawing the earth and plunging, they seem to rush directly out of the picture. Like good King Duncan's steeds of old,

> Beauteous and swift, the minions of their race
> Turn'd wild in nature, broke their stalls, flung out
> Contending against obedience, as they would make
> War with mankind!

—Shakespeare

What perfect understanding on the part of the artist is revealed in the study of each horse. Here in the foreground the gray draft horses pose in the highest light of the picture. With arching necks they are trotting with stately pace, measured and slow. Their glossy mottled coats fairly glow with mettle and fire. How composed they seem! How gallant is their bearing! How proudly they hold their shapely heads beneath the strain of the reins in the hands of that strong man upon the back of one of them! He is finding it hard, indeed, to hold in check such strength. See how the sinewy muscles of his great right arm stand out knotted and powerful. In his bearing there is evident pride in such matchless charges as these. Are not such,

> The true pearl of every caravan;
> The light and life of all our camps,—the force
> And glory of their clan?

—Sir F. H. Doyle

Rearing wildly, the black colt just behind, poses in the unruly and uncontrollable fire of youth. No less excited, the white horse at his side is plunging in a playful mood. We wonder at the courage of the guide seemingly carried off his feet by their wild actions. With eyes gleaming wickedly the colt is the one disturbing element of the group.

In contrast the little pony at his right is trotting meekly along without a guide. We can admire this animal for his good sense. A blanket is strapped to his back for safe keeping. It suggests a humbler mission here than that of his companions, possibly that of serving as a pack horse in the interest of the exhibition.

But what shall we say of this fine steed at the left trotting along so proudly and so gallantly? A poet once described such a horse when he said,

> A broad round back
> Has my favorite steed; his slender neck
> And head he tosses high.
>
> A war horse meet for warrior's need,
> That none who passed might choose but heed,
> So strong he stood, so great, so fair.

—Swinburne

While it is true that we are first of all impressed by the wonderful action of the splendid animals in this masterpiece, yet there is a deeper meaning which the artist would have us learn.

Longfellow has most beautifully expressed it in his *Psalm of Life*. Corot, that musician of the landscape, has bequeathed it to us in his pictures of fields, lakes and woodlands; Millet, in his humble toilers of the plain. But to Rosa Bonheur it was given, in this subject, to express anew, though in a different language and through a different medium, the same theme—the exaltation of God.

From Psalm CIV

O Lord, how manifold are Thy works! in wisdom hast Thou made them all : the earth is full of thy riches.

PLAN FOR STUDY

1. **Source of Subject.** The horse market, or horse fair, as it was commonly called, constitutes the subject of our study. Eighteen months of study were spent in preparation for the painting of this famous picture. Obtaining permission from the Prefect of Police, the artist adopted male attire and visited, to some extent unmolested, the Paris horse markets to study the animals on exhibition there. M. Dailly, manager of the Paris Omnibus Company, offered her the use of their powerful horses for these studies, even sending them to her studio where she might sketch them undisturbed. Each animal represents weeks of painstaking sketching.

2. **Setting.** The scene is a much-frequented part of Paris, probably a copy of the market on Boulevard de l'Hospital where the artist made many of her preparatory studies. The Dome of the Invalides is seen in the distance suggesting the busy city within whose precincts this market or fair is located. A fringe of young trees forms a pleasing natural background, behind which, one notes a suggestion of a track for speeding horses. But the powerful animals of Flemish stock on this side are evidently being led for inspection rather than for racing, there being a suggestion of spectators among the trees at the right, and also in this group before which the horse at the extreme right is being trotted.

The sunshine floods the picture with warmth and freshness which accord with the overflowing spirits of men and horses. There is even a suggestion of stir in the foliage. The rolled-up sleeves and unbuttoned collars of the men reveal the muscular strength that must cope with these fiery spirits. The flowing manes and tails, and the fluttering blouses are suggestive of rapid movement.

3. **Arrangement.** Some twenty or thirty horses are arranged with varying degrees of distinctness across the front of the canvas. Nine or ten of the most striking ones with their grooms are represented in detail in the near foreground, while behind and to the extreme right are more or less obscured

forms either hurrying in the general direction, or standing in rows for appraisement. One notes in the arrangement a rather ineffective grouping of models posing for effect. But others express views that are quite the contrary. For example, note the variety of types shown. Some are being ridden by powerful men whose knotted muscles show the effort required to hold them. Other grooms are nearly carried off their feet by the rearing and curveting of those they are leading. Here one meek little pony trots along quietly, and at his side a colt rears and prances under the severe beating his master is giving him. Here at the right where the ring turns, note the fine action of the gallant Percheron whose hind quarters only are visible. Everywhere there is a rush of numbers.

Observe the preponderance of the diagonal lines and their contribution to the impression of action; also the curved lines of the rounded forms of the horses, and lines that suggest movement. Observe the presence of the vertical lines in the trunks and branches of the trees on the right, balancing those of the dome on the left. The horizontal lines of the ground are repeated in the general line along the tops of the trees.

The characteristics of the Flemish type of horses in the broad, round backs, the powerful arching necks, and heavy hoofs, show a complete mastery of horse anatomy on the part of the artist. Note the masses of muscle on the hips and shoulders of the grays, on the terrified colt, and on yonder animal at the turn of the lane. Study the principle of perspective in the arrangement—the dome with its outline blurred through the atmosphere, the men at the extreme right in contrast with those in the foreground, and the suggestive strokes serving to represent in rows the horses being appraised.

4. **Center of Interest.** In representing a subject where so many individual types must needs be portrayed, the artist nevertheless preserved the unity of her composition by subordinating in more or less degree the majority of her figures. We easily see that she has emphasized the powerful draft team in the highest light of the picture. Our eye first studies them, then passes on to lesser details, yet all the while returning to the central figures. Note, too, how the center of

interest is placed on one side. With what is it balanced on the left?

The picture includes two classes or groups of horses, one representing the Flemish stock and the other the Arabian. Size and strength characterize those of Flemish stock. This breed of draft horses has been brought to a high degree of perfection in Perche, northern France, whence the name Percheron, as applied to these horses. In France they are used mainly for the artillery and for omnibus service in cities.

The chief characteristics of the Percheron are clearly and beautifully set forth by the artist in the dapple-grays in the foreground, whose every movement serves to show that they are conscious of their strength and beauty.

5. **Supreme Motive.** The artist painted animals because she loved them. For her, every animal had an individual character. The secret of her power in representing animals lay in her instinctive ability to read that character in her subjects. She never attributed human qualities to her animals, and though she truthfully represented their feelings as well as their forms, she never strove for sentiment. She aimed only to paint animals very true to nature, regarding her subjects beautiful and interesting to the degree in which they manifested the gentle or strong traits with which the Creator had endowed them.

6. **Light and Shade.** The light comes from the right, the sun, judging from the shadows, being well up in the sky. The brightest light on the forms of the foremost horses serves to concentrate our interest upon them. The landscape is very much subordinated to the figures, its chief purpose being merely to suggest the cause of this assembling of the horses. The original is remarkable for the dust glinting in the bright sunshine which prevails in the lower levels of the picture. "I love to catch the rapid motion of animals," the artist once said, "the reflection of light and color on their coats, their different characteristics (for every animal has its individual physiognomy)."

7. **History.** *The Horse Fair* was painted in the artist's studio at 56 Rue d' Assas, Paris, and was exhibited in the

Salon of 1853. The following history of the picture is gleaned from a letter written by Mr. Ernest Gambert to S. P. Avery. This picture came back to the painter unsold in 1858. Anxious that her native village of Bordeaux purchase it, the artist offered the picture to that municipality for $2,400. Failing in this she accepted the offer of Mr. Gambert, representing Gambert and company of England, receiving $8,000. The original being too large to be easily engraved, she kindly offered to make a small copy of it and delivered both to the purchaser for the same amount. The exhibition of the *Horse Fair* in England in 1855, created a great stir, the Queen herself requesting that it be brought to Windsor for her inspection. Mr. Jacob Bell purchased the small copy for $5,000 and presented it to the National Gallery. Mr. Wright, an American, about the same time secured the original for $6,000. In 1871 it was sold to A. T. Stewart, Waukeeken, New York, for $20,000, and at his death, 1887, Samuel Avery, acting for Mr. Cornelius Vanderbilt, bought it at auction for $55,500. The purchaser presented it to the Metropolitan Museum of Art, New York City, where it now hangs. A second copy was made by the artist and was sold for $5,000. A third replica in water color is owned in England. The original measures seven and three-quarter feet by sixteen and one-half feet. The horses are represented two-thirds lifesize.

COMMENT

Rosa Bonheur drives a tandem of Flemish horses through a square of canvas, and over the necks of her critics.—Dall

The *Horse Fair* has no doubt many striking points, and is without doubt the most important picture, so far as we know, ever painted by a woman. Its chief merit is its out-of-doors quality, and one of the horses, the Percheron at the extreme right, which is turning from the spectator, is a noble animal well painted.—Ernest Knauff

QUESTIONS

What is this picture about? How do these horses feel? Where are they being taken? Do they seem to want to go? Why do you think so? Can you see all of them quite dis-

tinctly? What are the men doing? What is the expression
on their faces? In what are they interested? Are they much
interested in one another? Can you find one man who shows
great strength? One who seems a trifle cruel? How are the
men dressed? What traits of character do their actions show?
Which horses seem very proud? Meek? Frightened? Angry?
Playful? Have you ever seen horses like these? Where?
What were they doing? Do these horses behave naturally?
In which are you most interested? Which do you think the
artist wanted to make the most important? Where is the
action taking place? In which are you the more interested,
the landscape, the surroundings, or the animals? Why? What
is the purpose of the landscape? What sounds do you seem
to hear? What actions do you seem to see? What are the
good qualities of some of the horses? What are some of the
best traits revealed here? Which are the most beautiful
horses? What are their beautiful qualities? Where is the
brightest light? From which direction does it come? What
is the one word which might describe this scene? What do
you think the artist is trying to tell us in it? What good
qualities of her character does the picture reveal?

THE ARTIST

Bonheur, *Bo ner'*, **Marie Rosalie** (1822—1899), the most celebrated woman painter of animals, was born at Bordeaux,
France. At an early age her father gave her instruction in
drawing, in which she displayed extraordinary talent. Notwithstanding her aptitude for art, she was compelled to learn
the trade of a dressmaker. Later her father, perceiving her
remarkable talent, allowed her to abandon dressmaking to de-
vote herself to art. She studied and sketched in and about
Paris. In 1841 she exhibited her *Rabbits Eating Carrots,*
which attracted wide attention. In 1848 and again in 1855
she was awarded a medal of the first class.

During the Franco-Prussian War her studio at By was left
undisturbed by special order of the Crown Prince of Prussia.
In 1849 she founded the Free School of Design for young girls

and was its director until her death. She was awarded the Cross of the Legion of Honor, and it was delivered in person by the Empress Eugenie. She exhibited at the World's Columbian Exposition at Chicago in 1893, and the following year was made an officer of the Legion of Honor. She died at her chateau at By, near Paris, in 1899.

Rosa Bonheur was fond of detail, and dwelt with lingering touches on the animal's hair or wool. Gentle movements were what suited her brush best. Her *Horse Fair*, with its greater animation, was an exception to the rule; and she can hardly be said to have produced another canvas like that.—Debat Ponson

PLOWING IN THE NIVERNAIS

Bonheur

Clear the brown path, to meet his coulter's gleam!
Lo! on he comes, behind his smoking team,
With toil's bright dew-drops on his sunburnt brow,
The lord of earth, the hero of the plow!

First in the fields before the reddening sun,
Last in the meadows when the day is done,
Line after line, along the bursting sod,
Marks the broad acres where his feet have trod.

.　.　.　.　.

True to their home, these faithful arms shall toil
To crown with peace their own untainted soil.

—Holmes, *The American Plowman*

THE PICTURE

A vast field, stretching for miles and miles to meet the sunny sky behind the misty veil of the distance, and here at the left swelling to the gentle slope of the hillside is nature's choicest setting for this interesting scene.

Two groups of six oxen each, moving two abreast with steps, measured and slow, draw the plows which are turning the field into furrows.

What splendid animals they are. As if proudly conscious of their strength, in their coats of white and brown the oxen move steadily forward. Here the first pair lead off with a show of great power. That they have all the qualities of leadership is seen at a glance. There is no shirking in their steady gait, no sign of weariness in their huge bodies, but rather a determination to reach a distant goal. Untold strength is revealed in the knotted muscles of shoulders and sides, and in the chain extending from yoke to yoke and drawn taut as they forge ahead with more than an equal share of the load.

120

PLOWING IN THE NIVERNAIS.—*Bonheur*

Just back of them a less energetic team pose in the full light of the picture. In direct contrast to the leaders these weary animals lag behind. But their faltering gait is noticed by the driver and with his goad he urges them forward. There is no help for it, they must go on. With mild protest in his eyes, the weary but patient animal nearest the driver moves a little faster. The other is not so inclined, and, somewhat rebellious, tosses his head with wildly glaring eyes.

The plowing is well advanced. Much of the field already lies in long, even furrows, fresh and steaming. An afternoon sun shines full upon the scene and speaks of the long hours that have passed. Nevertheless the work goes steadily on. The day has been warm and the men have thrown coats aside. Now the first team is trudging over a slight rise while just behind, the second has begun the ascent. We can almost see the smooth progress of the plowshare guided so skilfully by strong hands, as it turns the furrow. At the left the field swells to the gently sloping hillside bordered with its green hedge rows, where among the orchards nestle the cottages of the laborers.

Why, then, is this picture truly great? Wherein lies its charm? We answer that it is an heroic scene. But are there not great paintings, questions one, which give to us the heroism of battles, of jeweled thrones or of brilliant courts? Yes, but Nature in this scene is the "throned monarch" before whom all earthly kings must bow.

Perfectly contented, these peasants plow and sow and reap, while Nature rewards their labor with bountiful harvests from out her own great store. So is such toil heroic; so is this picture truly great.

PLAN FOR STUDY

1. **Source of Subject.** The opening lines of George Sand's *La Mare au Diable* (The Devil's Pool), in which is set down that author's conception of farm labor, are credited with being the source of Rosa Bonheur's inspiration for this subject. The artist's father, it is related, read the passage to the members

of his family about the evening lamp. "The plowman, young and robust," begins the celebrated paragraph, "The ground, rich, eight vigorous oxen, and a bright autumn sunlight lighting up the scene," closing with the author's comment, "It would be a fine subject for a painter." "Yes," Rosa is said to have replied at this point, "the author is right." Soon after, on the occasion of a visit in the vicinity of Nivernais with Madame Sand's description still in mind, she made studies of peasants at their customary labors in the fields, the result of which was this picture, exhibited in 1849.

2. **Setting.** A broad expanse of level land swelling at the left to the slope of the hillside is in general the natural setting. Observe the charm of the fresh out-of-doors quality of the landscape. The sky is bright, and against it the figures of the men and oxen stand out in rugged strength. The natural setting is one of repose, in which a spirit of sunniness, of cheery warmth is dominant. Note the deep sky which, one observes, always lends nobility to a picture. The scene affords opportunity to study primitive farming implements and methods: the rude, clumsy plowshare necessitating the combined strength of six oxen to turn a single furrow, in contrast with our modern gang plow and horses. One man guides the plow, another, with much goading and shouting, holds the oxen to the furrow. The suggestion of the laborers' homes on the hillside seems to furnish a motive for their industry.

3. **Arrangement.** First of all, let us look at the comparative spaces of sky and land. The chief figures are arranged in the right foreground, and starting with the first team of oxen on the right are followed by other pairs represented with varying degrees of distinctness across the picture. Four laborers accompany the animals, two men and six oxen being necessary to the progress of a single plow. Note the predominating horizontal lines, the undulating lines of furrow and field, as well as the slanting lines of goads and plows. The curved lines of the foliage and hillside break the monotony in the background; the rolling character of the field emphasizes the impression of action in the figures of the foreground. The slight rise just ahead of the first plow is strongly suggestive of an increased

effort on the part of the straining oxen ahead. The driver notes it too, and shouts and goads to prevent any lagging at this juncture. The furrows in the foreground show that the plowing is well advanced, but the field lying between the oxen and the hillside indicates that a good strong task is still ahead of the plowmen. The strain of the long hard pull up the slope is emphasized by the line passing along the backs of the oxen. Observe how the hillside in the background serves to balance this trend of lines. The entire scene is expressive of slow cumbersome progress, nevertheless a progress that is active and constant.

4. **Center of Interest.** Our interest centers on the foremost team of oxen, because of their position and size. Observe that the other figures, both men and oxen, are subordinated. Even the driver with the foremost team does not detract from the interest centered upon them. Note the lighting in emphasizing this center of interest. As has been pointed out, the landscape, while charming and interesting, is subordinated to the central thought of service.

5. **Supreme Motive.** There was a dignity and a nobility about the labor of the fields that appealed to the soul of Madame Bonheur, and this she has admirably expressed in this picture. She was a close student of nature. Moreover, her knowledge of animals was greater than that of any other woman painter. The toil of the farm-laborer, so constant a companion of nature, and the patient and strong effort of these oxen naturally made a strong appeal to her. While her conception cannot be called a poetic one, her treatment seldom taking sentiment into account, yet in this scene we feel that we are given an unusually grand expression of the eternal fitness of honest, humble toil. Speaking of this characteristic of her work, Victor Hugo says:

> The boldness of her conception is sublime. As a creative artist I place her first among women living or dead. And if you ask me why she towers above her fellows, by the majesty of her work silencing every detractor, I will say it is because she listens to God, and not to man. She is true to herself.

6. **Light and Shade.** The light comes from the left, and the shadows indicate that the sun is well up in the sky. It is the

sunny quality of the subject which proves its chief charm. Note how the play of muscles is brought out by the lighting, and how strongly the figures stand out against the gray of the field and the sky. Observe the impression of strain in the legs rounded out against the dark of the shadows and how the hoofs sink into the soft earth and take hold of it as the oxen move up the furrow. ''The very earth smokes, while there is a decided sense of moisture in the overturned soil.''

7. **Color.** The cool, restful colors always dominant in a natural spring landscape form the ground note of the scene. The white, brown and cream-colored oxen; the rich, reddish-brown tones of the earth; the broad field and hillside with varying shades of brown, gray and green all under a sunny blue sky, give the subject a coloring both delicate and harmonious.

8. **History.** This picture was begun in the winter of 1848, and was exhibited the following year at the Salon, where it met with great success. Because of a lack of funds the French Minister of Fine Arts could only offer the artist the ridiculously low sum of $600 for it. This she accepted, and the picture became the property of Luxembourg Gallery, Paris. The artist's father was on his death bed when word came of his daughter's first success. Asking to see the work, the painting was shown him as he lay there, whereupon he expressed great happiness and satisfaction. A replica, now possibly owned in America, was sold to M. Mare for $500. The original is four feet four inches high, and six feet nine inches wide.

Its beauty lies in its absolute truth.—Prince Stirbey

This painting so true to nature, so well drawn, so carefully modeled and so harmonious in color, at once established her reputation as a great artist.—Bouguereau

QUESTIONS

What are these men doing? How many do you see? Is the same work done by all? What are these animals that draw the plow? Have you ever seen any? Where? What were they doing? Have you ever seen them doing this sort of work? Were they ever used in this country? When? Where? Which

team are the best workers? Which are the lazy ones? Which
draw the greatest part of the load? How does the artist show
this? Are the plows hard to pull? How does the artist show
this? Where do these men live? Do they seem to be willing
workers? How does the artist make us feel this? Where does
the light come from? How are you able to tell? What sounds
do you seem to hear? What actions do you seem to see? What
seem to be the traits of these oxen? What are their good qualities? In what are you most interested, the men, the oxen or
the landscape? Why? Which do you feel the artist wanted
to make the most important? Why? What is the spirit of the
landscape? What one thing does the artist seem to say in this
picture? What were her feelings do you think, when she
painted the scene? What thoughts do you have as you study
it? What features of the picture appeal to you most?

> Haply from them the toiler, bent
>   Above his force or plow, may gain
> A manlier spirit of content,
>   And feel that life is wisest spent
> Where the strong working hand makes
>   Strong the working brain.
>   —Whittier. *Songs of Labor*

LANDING OF THE PILGRIMS

Rothermel

Wild was the day; the wintry sea
  Moaned sadly on New England's strand,
When first the thoughtful and the free,
  Our fathers, trod the desert land.
They little thought how pure a light,
  With years, should gather round that day;
How love should keep their memories bright,
  How wide a realm their sons should sway.

—Bryant, 22d of December

THE PICTURE

The Pilgrims were to sail. Such bustle and excitement over the departure of a ship the English village of Plymouth had never seen. The sun had scarcely risen when from the homes whole families gathered at the seashore.

Out on the waves the good ship *Mayflower* rode at anchor. Such a glorious day. Fields, woods and the sea reflected the warm glow of an Autumn sun, while Autumn breezes fresh with fragrance and promise of harvest swept the shore and the gleaming water.

Only the sad and tearful faces of the people as they were rowed to the ship did not respond to the brightness of the morning. Sorrowful and very trying was the parting hour. On board the vessel the good Pastor Robinson, encouraging and consoling, moved among his people. All forgetful of their own sorrows, brave leaders that they were, Bradford, Standish, Brewster and Carver dispelled many a shadow with their beaming faces and words of cheer. Neighbors clasped hands with neighbors for the last time, while friends took leave of friends with tearful farewells.

Who were these Pilgrims? Why this sorrow over their departure? Ah! it was indeed a great day in this village and in the history, too, not only of our own country but of the world as well.

Years before there had come to the throne of England a king who set up a powerful church. Indeed an order went out over all the land compelling everyone to worship in it. In the little town of Scrooby, a band of Christian folk resolved not to heed this law. They did not believe in this king's church, and above all they were determined to worship God in the way they thought right. But the king was powerful, his officers were many, and terrible indeed were some of the experiences of these people. They met and worshipped in secret and were thrown into prison for it. Their homes were watched day and night while sometimes their leaders were put to death.

There came a time, however, when even such patient men and women as these could endure the persecution no longer. They resolved to sail to Holland where everyone, so they had heard, had perfect freedom in their worship. They went to this land and lived there happily for twelve years.

But even as the birds of our own northern states feel in the autumn that unrest and longing for the brighter land of sunshine and flowers, so these Pilgrims longed too, for a home where their children might live as Englishmen in a new land of peace and freedom to worship God.

But a few weeks before one of their own countrymen had written from far-off America, describing the country as far more beautiful than England, with game and forests in abundance. To this promising land the Pilgrim Fathers decided to go.

On board the last farewell was spoken. The sails were flung to the wind. The *Mayflower* rode slowly out of the harbor. Fortunate it was that the merry voices of children relieved the first sorrowful moments. When the last familiar line of shore was lost to view and sorrowful, serious thoughts engaged all on board, *Old Hundred*, from a hundred throats, filled the ship with inspiring song. One verse followed another until the last refrain was reached, and then as if all trouble,

LANDING OF THE PILGRIMS.—*Rothermel*

care and sadness melted away before the calm, holy peace of hearts, they chanted "For the Lord is good; His mercy is everlasting; and His truth endureth to all generations."

Day after day passed. Sometimes the sun was hidden behind black, threatening storm-clouds. Great waves swept the deck and heavy gales tossed the vessel about as if she were a toy.

Many weeks thus slipped away and the snow flurries of the Christmas month gathered about. Then over the water were wafted the odors of pine, oak and sassafras. Land birds circled the ship, while dimly outlined in the mist, were the bleak shores and dark forests of the new world.

A cold, snowy day dawned for the landing. Even nature seemed determined to test the courage and faith of these people. Freezing winds blew in strong gusts while white-capped waves dashed against the vessel and the great rocks of the shore.

The boat was lowered. To and fro it was rowed between ship and landing place. Upon the frozen snow in darkness the Pilgrims knelt. *Old Hundred* again sounded forth and mingled with the roar of the ocean.

Know ye that the Lord is God; it is He that hath made us; not we ourselves; we are His people and the sheep of His pasture.

We need only to view the setting and action of this painting to realize for ourselves the daring and heroism of the Pilgrim Fathers. Huge waves are tossed against the frail boat and rocky shore as if to destroy them. Storm clouds darken the sky, while the dashing waves and flying draperies portray the force of the wind. In the darkness at the right is a suggestion of the forest, and in the foreground snow covered, rocky shore makes a firm landing place.

It requires the combined strength of stalwart oarsmen to hold the boat close to the rock. The rope in the hands of the man in the foreground seems stretched almost to the breaking point. It is as if the waves were making one last great effort to swallow up boat, people and landing place.

See how the foot of this man to the right is braced against a jagged rock in the foaming surf. Every muscle of his body is braced for this supreme endeavor. The strong hand grasps the rope firmly as the boat is steadied to allow the women to step ashore.

Our interest naturally centers upon the two figures in the central foreground. Here in the brave, anxious face of the woman and in the dauntless type of her companion is expressed the real character of the Pilgrims. They have begun life in a new land under conditions that will test to the utmost their spirit of courage, of faith and devotion. Yet there is no trace of weakness in the stalwart figure of the man. Braced on the solid rock he is concerned just now with the safe landing of the passengers. We share with his beautiful companion her anxiety; but we have utmost confidence in the strong arm reached out to help her. In the boat two companions await their turn with anxious, though determined expressions.

Behind them another strong form completes the group in the foreground. With arms outstretched and pole held firmly, he, too, is bracing the boat. In the stern are other oarsmen. The action of the upright figure bracing the boat with a rope fastened on shore completes the line of bodily effort.

No less interesting is the group waiting on the shore. Here in the center a husband and wife kneel in prayer. In the earnest devout expression of the man standing in the midst we are led to feel the character of the good elder of the little congregation. Does not the commanding figure of the man at his left suggest Miles Standish?

Indistinct in the darkness of the background are other men and women in various attitudes of praise and worship. In the distance dimly outlined against the lowering storm clouds the *Mayflower* rides.

For these people the future seems dark indeed. The woods so near at hand harbor wild animals and roaming Indians of which they know but little. A terrible winter looks them in the face, and, ah well, perhaps it is best they cannot know that next summer's flowers will bloom on the graves of half their little band, because they chose to set in the bleak New England coast the precious jewel of liberty. Why were the Pilgrims truly great? Because their mission was a heroic one.

Aye, call it holy ground,
　　The soil where first they trod.
They have left unstained what there they found
　　Freedom to worship God.

　　　　　　　　　　　　—Felicia Hemans

PLAN FOR STUDY

Since the merit of this painting lies almost wholly in its historical value, and not in its standing as a work of art, the intensive study of setting, arrangement and motive is omitted. The questions for study, however, have been designed to develop a satisfactory study of the composition.

The Pilgrim Fathers. The leaders were:

John Robinson, pastor of the congregation at Scrooby, Amsterdam and Leyden. He did not, however, accompany his people to America.

William Brewster, ruling elder of the church in Leyden, as well as in New Plymouth.

John Carver, first governor of the Plymouth Colony.

John Alden, immortalized in Longfellow's *Courtship of Miles Standish*. He is said to have been the first to step on the Plymouth Rock, although that honor has sometimes been accorded Mary Chilton. He was a magistrate in the colony fifty years, and outlived all other signers of the Mayflower Compact.

Miles Standish, the subject of Longfellow's poem. He was appointed captain of the Pilgrims in New Plymouth and undertook several expeditions against the Indians.

QUESTIONS

Who are these people? What are they doing? Do you know the story of the Pilgrims? Why did they leave their native country? What season of the year is shown in this picture? What time of day? How many people do you see? Are they all doing the same thing? What is the expression on their faces? Compare their expressions? Where is strength shown? In what persons are you most interested? Where does your interest center first? Where is the brightest light? The darkest spot? What is this man nearest us doing? Who helps him steady the boat? What qualities of character are expressed in these people? What purpose leads them to come to this strange shore? What thoughts do you have as you view the scene? In what are you most interested, the people or the landscape? Why? What is the chief thing the artist is trying to tell us? What do you like best about the picture? What part of it do you think will remain longest in your memory?

THE ARTIST

Roth'ermel, Peter Frederick (1817—1895), an American historical painter, was born at Nescopack, Pa. He was a pupil of Bass Otis in Philadelphia, and began his career as a painter of portraits, but soon changed to historical subjects. From 1847 to 1855 he was director of the Pennsylvania Academy. He then spent two years in Europe studying the works of the great masters. Rothermel painted many pictures, a number of which are of historical importance, Art critics consider that he had talent for composition but lacked technical ability. Some of his most noted pictures are: *Columbus Before Queen Isabella, The Christian Martyrs, The Battle of Gettysburg, De Soto Discovering the Mississippi,* and *Patrick Henry Before the House of Burgesses.*

JOAN OF ARC

Bastien-Lepage

But ah, the Visions and the Voices, Lord!
  Thy heaven is all a flashing of white fire
And every angel bears a flaming sword
  Calling me forth . . . Lord, if at Thy desire
I must put by the distaff and the wheel,
  I am Thy handmaid . . . make me unto France
A heart of adamant and edge of steel
  Like Deborah of old. Cry the advance!
          —Charles B. Going, *Joan of Arc at Domremy*

THE PICTURE

There has always been intermarrying among the royal families of Europe. As a result, it occasionally happens that the heir to the throne of one country is a member of the royal family of another country. During the Middle Ages there were a number of conflicting claims to the thrones of France and England, and in every case the countries tried to settle these claims by war. The Hundred Years' War, begun in 1338 by Edward II of England, was one of these conflicts that lasted for more than a century. The English won several important victories, the last at Agincourt under Henry V.

Now at the close of a century of battles which history calls the Hundred Years' War, English troops were besieging the last stronghold of France, the city of Orleans. With a lost cause confronting them, soldiers deserting their arms, and their gentle king about to abandon the throne, it was no wonder that the people became discouraged. How despairing was that call of a sorely troubled nation, the call for a man; a man of dauntless courage, with a steady arm and a pure heart, one who could lead them to victory!

134

JOAN OF ARC.—*Bastien Lepage*

Not far from Orleans in the little hamlet of Domremy there lived a young peasant maid. To her the wrongs heaped upon her native country seemed like the cruel stings of the lash. Out in the pleasant fields nestled between the vast forests of the Vosges, alone with her sheep, she prayed that her country and king might be saved.

Joan was a pious girl, seldom at play and often to be found praying in the village church. Truly hers was a strange childhood. From her mother's lips, as they sat under the blossoming apple trees in the pleasant garden, she heard the inspiring legends of her country; legends of war and its cruelty, and legends of her beloved saints. The mystery of the woods and fields, and these stories fired her imagination. In the little church which sheltered her father's cottage, the pictured faces of the saints looked down upon her from their golden frames. Taking the form of visions, they entreated her to "free her country from the invaders."

One summer day when the old oak forest had never seemed so mysterious, Joan sat humming softly as she spun. Suddenly a light filled the place with a heavenly glow. Saintly women clad in white robes and crowned with jewels and garlands of flowers appeared among the branches. Sweet voices bade her "Go to the aid of the king and thou shalt restore his kingdom." Joan replied, "I know not how to ride or lead men to arms." "Go," they called again, "go and the Lord be with you."

From the little home, the sunny garden and the sheltering church walls, Joan went out to the aid of her king. With an enthusiasm and courage born of a faith in God, she braved the dangers of miles of trackless forests, and came to the royal palace. There in the presence of the gayest and most polite court in the whole world, she bowed before the youthful ruler and received his consent to lead the armies of France.

Clad in pure white armor and mounted on a powerful black charger Joan hurried to Orleans. Of Napoleon it was said, "His presence added to the army a hundred thousand men;" but the inspired Joan brought with her the force of twice a hundred thousand.

With renewed courage, and with spirits aroused to the highest pitch, the troops of Orleans followed the white-armored maid through the city gates. On to the river Loire they advanced in solid ranks, with cheers that awoke the distant hills. On to the very walls of the enemy's watch towers rushed Joan of Arc, bearing the white standard high aloft and the sword of Saint Catherine unsheathed and flashing in the sunlight, pointing to the distant gate. A sea of faces, a perfect wall of humanity greeted the astonished English. Never had such enthusiasm been witnessed. In the face of it, they fled in dismay. The siege was lifted, and France was saved to her King.

The little shepherdess, the peasant daughter of Lorraine, had accomplished that which all the powerful, chivalrous manhood of France had failed to do. She also led the French to victory at Patay, June 18, 1429, and assisted at the coronation of Charles VII at Rheims. In 1430 she was captured by the English, condemned as a heretic and burned at the stake the following year.

To Bastien-Lepage, who lived as a boy near her home, the stirring story of Joan of Arc was an impressive one. He resolved to represent her, not as the refined, beautiful woman which she had often been represented, but as a simple peasant in the humble environment of her girlhood.

The spirit of spring, of warmth and sunshine breathes from the natural setting. The branches with their clusters of pink apple blossoms scattered plentifully among the green leaves must be much like those in the old garden of Domremy. The gray soil splotched with light, the tangle of wild flowers, and the green carpet of grass are pictured in minutest detail.

Who can tell the thoughts of this maiden as she sat winding yarn in the shadow of the apple trees. What emotions must have thrilled her as she thought of her country's wrongs. Of a sudden a bright light floods the garden. Quickly rising, overturning the spinning wheel in her haste, she advances with outstretched hands, in answer to the call she has heard. With what a thrill of wonder she sees the spirits of the saints she so well knows shaping themselves from the mist and light.

"Go to the aid of the king," the voices say. As suddenly
as they came they vanish in the mists as the girl dreams on.

The garden with its trees, its cottage and its flowers is lost
as we study the face of Joan. Truly has it been said that
"eyes are mirrors of the soul," and truly the soul of the peasant girl looks out of eyes gazing far beyond all earthly things
into the very light of heaven itself. The voices of saints are
calling her to service. There is a submission, gentle and trust-
ful in character, which will lead her to follow their bidding
at any cost.

PLAN FOR STUDY

1. **Source of Subject.** Joan of Arc (French Jeanne d'Arc),
whose story is told in the preceding pages, is the subject of the
picture.

In connection with this discussion of the source of the subject, Prince Karageorgevitch, a personal friend of the artist's,
relates the following: "One day, I remember, he saw his
mother returning fatigued from the fields. She kept seeing
before her some thistles which she had looked at too long in
the corn, whereat Bastien-Lepage was at first much alarmed.
The son tended the mother until at last the painter began to
take a deep interest in the thing. He questioned his mother,
asking her to tell him all she saw, whether the thistles appeared to her as actual objects, or if she saw them only when
she closed her eyes. But it was really a vision that she had
had—a curious optical illusion that had the appearance of
reality. On the green in front of their house, she saw again
the thistles quite big, close to her, gradually getting smaller
as they receded, and while her own son still spoke to her she
saw them. This idea haunted the painter's mind, and was to
suggest a great picture to him.

"From it arose the idea of *Jeanne d'Arc*, his masterpiece.
The painter made a journey to Domremy, the little village
where Jeanne d'Arc was born. He saw the heroine's house,
pictured to himself in his mind's eye the scene of the vision,
and then at once set to work."

2. **Setting**. The detail in this setting is rendered with photographic accuracy. But this cannot be said to be to the merit of the composition. A biographer tells us that Bastien-Lepage made a special trip to Domremy to paint Joan's garden. It was characteristic of the man to set down with accuracy what he saw, so much so, that, unlike Millet and Corot and others, he set up his easel in the spot he was to represent and reproduced it exactly. A camera would do the same thing. But such a reproduction is not true art.

An artist may represent natural scenes in two ways. He may be susceptible to the spirit, and the impression which plays upon his heart strings, and seek to reflect it in his painting; or he may represent only the visible appearance. If he chooses the first and builds well, his work will arouse in the beholder much the same emotion that he felt when he himself saw the original scene. But a painting after the second manner can never inspire true sentiment. Just to that extent it fails of being a really great work of art.

Here is where Bastien-Lepage's painting meets its severest criticism. The setting confuses with its detail. Is there a dominating impression in the setting? Should there not be? It is true that the leaves and blossoms on the outermost twigs are rendered with exactness. Yet if we examine the leaves, we do not see the trees, and if we are forced to consider a multitude of details we cannot grasp the setting as a whole. Note the suggestion of Joan's occupation in the overturned stool and the wheel.

3. **Arrangement.** Critics are generally agreed that the location of the vision detracts. The artist himself explained its position by relating that the original canvas did not admit of a vision, and that he introduced it by sewing on new canvas. As it is, Joan's vision is indicated by vague figures of Saint Michael in armor, who holds a sword which he extends toward her; Saint Catherine with her hands clasped; and Saint Margaret, who is weeping. The chief figure by its position and size clearly dominates the scene.

4. **Center of Interest.** If the setting is disappointing the center of interest may be said to entirely offset it. True to

her type, the maid of Orleans is here represented as a working woman. The hands are coarse and speak of manifold daily duties. Her dress is the plain peasant garb. But the face. Where in art have we seen such a face? "His *Joan of Arc* of the Museum," says Mr. Preyer, "has that resigned, bewildered, semi-hypnotic, vaguely and yet intensely longing, spiritual expression which is worth all the biographies that ever were written of the Maid of Orleans." Writes Prince Karageorgevitch, "Her eyes, wide open and very bright, light up her face, making of the peasant girl a superior being. The poise is exquisitely true."

"Of all human phases of expression which painting can approach," says Muther, "such mystical delirium is perhaps the hardest to render; and probably it was only by the aid of hypnotism, to which the attention of the painter was directed just then, by the experiments of Charcot, that Bastien-Lepage was enabled to produce in this model that look of religious rapture, oblivious to the whole world, which is expressed in the vague glare of her eyes, blue as the sea."

5. **History.** *Joan of Arc* is signed in the artist's own hand, "J. Bastien-Lepage, Damvillars Manse, 1879." It was exhibited in the Salon of 1880. It was purchased from the artist for Mr. Erwin Davis, and given by him to the Metropolitan Museum, New York City, 1889. In that same year it was lent to the Exposition Universelle, Paris. It is on canvas, size eight feet four inches high by nine feet three inches wide.

It is nine years since I saw this picture at the Salon, and the deep impression it made on me seems to date from yesterday.—Karageorgevitch

QUESTIONS

What is the nature of this setting? In what to your mind does its real merit consist? Is your impression of the setting a single, definite one? Compare with respect to the motive, this setting with one of Millet's, Breton's or Corot's. What is the essential difference? Which constitutes real art? Account for the visions. What characterizes the center of interest? What is her type? What to your mind seems to be the artist's conception of the Maid of Orleans? Is it a pleasing one? Why? What is her expression? What qualities of character does she reveal? What feeling does the picture awaken in you? Is there any indication of traits of the painter's character here? What, for example?

THE ARTIST

Bastien-Lepage, *Bäs tyan' Lé päzh'*, **Jules** (1848—1884), a French painter, was born at Damvillars, France. He was a pupil of Cabanel, with whom he remained until 1870. He supported himself for a time by working for illustrated papers. His portrait of his grandfather, a success at the Salon of 1874, won him wide recognition. He received a third class medal in that year; a second class medal in 1875.

The artist, perhaps, was excelled by no one in his passionate love of nature. The healthy atmosphere and the picturesque scenery of woods and fields were accurately pictured by him.

Jules Bastien-Lepage deservedly ranks among the foremost in the modern movement of painting.—Preyer

He was impressionable to everything: the dangerous looking tramp that hung about one day near his father's house; the wood-cutter groaning beneath his burden; the passer-by, trampling the fresh grass of the meadows and leaving his trace behind him; the little sickly girl minding her lean cow upon a wretched field. That was what he wanted to paint, and that is what he painted. The life of the peasants of Lorraine is the theme of all his pictures, the landscape of Lorraine is their setting. He painted what he loved, and he loved what he painted.—Muther

THE NIGHT WATCH

Rembrandt

For in this land of Heaven's peculiar grace,
The heritage of nature's noblest race,
There is a spot of earth supremely blest,
A dearer, sweeter spot than all the rest,
Where man, creation's tyrant, casts aside
His sword and scepter, pageantry and pride,
While in his softened looks benignly blend
The sire, the son, the husband, brother, friend.

—Montgomery, Our Country

THE PICTURE

Differences between Charles V of Spain and the people of Netherlands and the severe measures adopted towards them by his son and successor, Philip II, led in 1579 to the federation of the northern provinces of that country into the Seven United Provinces of Netherlands. This federation was the beginning of the Dutch Republic, but it led to a war which continued until 1609, when the independence of these northern provinces was virtually acknowledged and peace was restored. But some of the military organizations were continued, among them the civic guards. These were reorganized to maintain the order of the cities in time of peace. Beautiful public buildings were erected for their places of assembly. Halls and grounds were provided for their training. To the patriotic people these military companies which had fought so valiantly and well in battle represented all that was praiseworthy. So it became the custom of wealthy citizens to perpetuate the memory of these brave men by placing their portraits in public buildings.

In the quaint old city of Amsterdam, there was maintained

THE NIGHT WATCH.—*Rembrandt*

a company of these guards known throughout all Holland for the wealth and influence of its membership. Its captain was Frans Banning Cocq, owner of a vast estate. Responding to the prevailing custom, this worthy group desired to have its portrait painted. Accordingly an artist from a neighboring city who had ten years before distinguished himself by painting *An Anatomy Lesson* was summoned before the company and given the commission.

When the request for this picture came to the artist, he resolved that his painting should be an inspiring message, a real lesson in patriotism, rather than a mere portrait of the guard. He saw in such a subject the years of struggle endured by his fatherland, and with little regard for the features of the men he painted, he worked for one year upon the picture. In 1642 it was unveiled before the astonished and indignant company.

With swords, muskets, pikes and helmets flashing in the glow of an afternoon sun, the brave men of the Amsterdam guard are pouring out of the drill hall in astonishing numbers, responding to a sudden call to arms.

In a uniform of black velvet, adorned with a red sash, the brave Captain Cocq is leading the way. At his side walks his lieutenant, van Ruytenburg. Clad in yellow coat and breeches, a yellow hat with plumes upon his head and a broad white scarf about his waist, he presents a striking contrast to his captain in black. Engaged in thoughtful, earnest conversation, these two move forward, unmindful of the haste and bustle about them.

Receding in a somewhat triangular arrangement with the glittering lights and bright colors of their costumes arrayed against the half light, the shadows, and the darkness, are the other members. How full of life they seem.

The drummer on the right is industriously beating out the alarm call. Balancing the foreground on the left is a figure in a red uniform and white scarf loading a musket. How lifelike, how real seems his act.

The inspiring drumbeats seem to give the standard-bearer new strength, for high aloft he is waving the bright-colored

banner of Amsterdam. Behind, rush the enthusiastic members
of the guard. In front surge troops of men from the dark
shadows of the doorway. To the right and behind the drummer
another squad is advancing, commanded by a sergeant who
is gravely pointing the way, and dimly outlined in the thick-
ening shadows, plumes and helmets speak of others who are
joining in the sortie.

Strange figures darting here and there, odd in stature and
quaintly costumed, add to the general animation of the scene.
In startling contrast, between the black of the captain's uniform and the red garb of the musketeer, flashes a strange little
vision. A pale green dress bedecked with jewels gives to the
child an unearthly appearance. Courtesying with a queenly
air, she stands among the hurrying soldiers for reasons un-
known. Some think that she is the captain's daughter, others
see in her the bearer of the alarm which has called out the
company. Undoubtedly it was the purpose of the artist to
introduce her as a bright light between two dark spots. A
street urchin darts between her and the captain, presumably
carrying a powder horn.

It is impossible to comprehend the astonishment of the men
of the guard when this painting was shown them. In vain they
searched for a glimpse of their features upon the canvas, then
vented their fury upon the painter, whose explanation that
he had tried something new, that a real picture with a real
message was to be preferred to a series of portraits, was useless.
The indignant men refused to consider the motive of an artist
who would obscure in shadow a man's face, that a witchlike
child might stand out in full light.

The picture was hung on the blackened walls of the armory,
where it remained unnoticed for years while the smoke of
countless Dutchmen's pipes and fumes from peat fires formed
a black crust upon the glowing colors.

Meanwhile a new town hall had been erected and *The Night
Watch* and several other pictures were taken from the old
armory to decorate the walls. *The Night Watch* was too large
for the place selected for it, between two windows, and was
cut down.

PLAN FOR STUDY

1. **Source of Subject.** A sortie of Captain Frans Banning Cocq's military company of Amsterdam is the subject. Sixteen members of the guard had each paid one hundred guilders to be represented life size in the picture.

2. **Setting.** The scene is above the steps and court of the Doelen of the Arquebusiers in Amsterdam, Holland, about the middle of the seventeenth century. Swords, muskets, pikes, helmets, uniforms, a drummer and a standard-bearer are all suggestive of the exciting moment when the guard was called out.

3. **Arrangement.** The twenty-nine members of the guard are portrayed in action in a somewhat triangular arrangement. Captain Cocq and his lieutenant in accordance with their rank are the chief figures in the foreground. The drummer, standard-bearer and queer little girl are more or less subordinated to the chief figures by their positions in the background. On the other hand, the majority of the men can hardly be distinguished in the shadow. Their faces, however, are intended for portraits and are carefully distinguished in the original by their names on an accompanying plate.

The whole composition conveys one definite impression. The vertical lines give the idea of power, dignity, solemnity and deliberation; in this scene they are in action. The figure of the little girl alone serves to break the monotony of the up-and-down lines. The diagonal, indicative of action and speed, is emphasized in the direction of the halberds, the flagstaff and the musket in the foreground. We also find the line of continuity and unity, beginning with the curve of the body of the musketeer at the left and extending around the picture the suggestion of an ellipse. Note evidences of balance in the arrangement—the drummer with the musketeer, the standard on the left with the prominent halberd on the right, the glare of light in the foreground with the luminous figure of the girl, etc.

4. **Center of Interest.** The figures of the captain and lieutenant at once attract our attention; the central thought, how-

ever, is the spirit and action of the men. The beating of the drum, the lifelike action of the musketeer and the waving of the standard all unite to give this impression. The easy, dignified bearing of the chief figures in the midst of a company of excited men, impresses the observer with their consciousness of the power which they have over their followers. The men may be reckless and prone to act rashly, but the calm, steady control of the leaders will easily keep them within bounds.

5. **Light and Shade.** The lighting is one of the notable qualities of the painting. Such work as this earned for the artist the title, "Prince of Shadows." We observe that unity in this composition is secured chiefly by the peculiar searchlight method of illumination. This is Rembrandt's original style of lighting. The light is confined principally to the faces, the bright spots being strongly emphasized by the mass of shadows about them. Rembrandt had a very perplexing problem in this painting. Sixteen men had each paid a little over forty dollars to have their portraits painted. Naturally each man expected to be represented with equal prominence.

A group picture of a number of individuals was in that period rather rare and expensive. To represent with skill and care each individual would be the natural course of the artist who sought goodwill and reputation. But such a picture could never be a true work of art. There would be no connecting link—no single, binding motive among the individuals of the group. Each would be concerned only with himself. His neighbor on either side would have no share of his thoughts. On the other hand, Rembrandt, the artist, was stirred by a strong, patriotic motive. He saw possibilities for the expression of a supreme idea in such a subject, but to accomplish this, unfortunately for the majority of the men of the guard, certain figures must of necessity be emphasized and others must be subordinated. Who can calculate the strength of purpose which influenced him to sacrifice wealth and reputation in his resolve to paint a truly great picture?

Under *Arrangement* we learned how unity was partially effected. But imagine the triangular arrangement with the full glare of an afternoon sun upon it. Every detail would be then equally emphasized and we would not be impressed at a first glance with the inspiring action of the men. No, rather our eyes would pass from face to face, from detail to detail, hither and thither, much as we scan the faces in a group photograph, with the result that no definite, single impression would be gained. In this canvas, the most effective means of securing unity is the lighting. Note the effect of the shadows also in adding to the mystery and solemnity of the scene. The highest light is massed on the chief forms.

6. **Supreme Idea.**

> Our watchword be—''Our native land!''
> Our motto—''Love forever!''
> My patriot brother.
>
> Patriots, in peace, assert the people's right,
> With noble stubbornness resisting might.
>
> —Dryden

7. **Color.**

Reds, yellows and blues, with buffs, saffrons, pearl grays, sapphires and opalescent tints run through it. . . . It is a wonder of color.—Van Dyke

There are gleams of gold and silver, moonlight-colored reflections, fiery lights; personages which like the girl with the blonde tresses, seem to shine by a light of their own; faces that seem lighted by the fire of conflagration; dazzling scintillations, shadows, twilight and deep darkness, all are there, harmonized and contrasted with marvelous boldness and insuperable art.—Amicis

8. **History.** We have already explained the origin of the picture and told where it was first hung. It was finally removed to Ryk's Museum, Amsterdam.

The picture has been known by several titles—*Sortie of the Civic Guard, Sortie of Captain Frans Banning Cocq's Company,* and *The Night Watch.* The last title was given by French writers of the eighteenth century because they thought the picture represented a night scene lighted by torches. This impression was probably due to the fact that through a long period of neglect the picture had become blackened by dirt and soot. In 1889 the curator of the museum had the canvas cleaned. It was then evident that the light came from the afternoon sun. Accordingly *Sortie of the Civic Guard* is the title now considered the most appropriate. The picture represents the guard as they are coming from the hall, at about four in the afternoon.

It is ranked by some critics as one of the Twelve World Pictures.

COMMENT

By its originality of treatment *The Night Watch* stands alone in the history of corporation pictures.—M. Michel

The Night Watch is . . . the greatest painting in the world, because it is the perfect, most harmonious union of idealism and realism ever reached.—Preyer

It has been raised to the skies as a wonder of the world, and pronounced unworthy of Rembrandt, discussed, interpreted, explained in a thousand ways and senses. But in spite of censure, conflicting judgments, it has been there for two centuries, triumphant and glorious; and the more you look at it, the more it is alive and glowing; and even seen only at a glance, it remains forever in the memory, with all its mystery.—Amicis

I do not know enough of art to say why it seems to me the most wonderful of the wonderful pictures, but its lights and shadows, its mysteries of distances and depths, its breathless humanness, give me the consciousness of immortal greatness.—Margaret Deland

QUESTIONS

What course of events probably inspired the artist in painting this subject? Why did the picture fail to please the men for whom it was painted? What would the artist have been forced to sacrifice in order to paint a picture that would have pleased them? Do you clearly understand this distinction? What is the essential quality of a truly great picture? Does this one appeal to the eye or to the emotions? What is the

probable occasion that it represents? Where are the chief
figures? How are they emphasized? How are the majority
of the forms subordinated? What in the picture contributes
to the impression of action, animation? What essential qualities distinguish the leaders? What lines predominate? What
is their significance in the giving of a definite impression?
Point out various examples of balance in the composition.
What does the lighting accomplish? Is it usual or unusual?
Is the lighting effective? How? Where is the source of the
light? What mistake did earlier critics make in regard to it?
What types of character do you find revealed in the attitudes
of the various men that are rendered distinctly? What is the
one definite impression that the artist wishes to give in this
subject? What helped you to determine this? What definite
impression will you carry with you after a study of this picture? What are its distinctive qualities? Its beautiful qualities? Its unusual qualities? What does it reveal about the
character of the artist?

THE ARTIST

Rembrandt, *Rem'bränt,* **Harmenszoon van Rijn** (1606—1669),
most distinguished painter and etcher of the Dutch School of
painting, was born at Leyden. His father was a wealthy mill
owner, and decided that this son should be educated for a
profession. But young Rembrandt's artistic proclivities were
so strong that at the age of twelve he was allowed to become
a pupil of van Swanenburch, in his native city. Three years
later he entered the studio of Pieter Lastman in Amsterdam.
In 1623 he returned to Leyden and remained until 1631, when
he removed to Amsterdam, where he passed the remainder of
his life.

Rembrandt at once became the first portrait painter of the
city. He also acquired great skill as an etcher. In 1634 he
married, and purchased a beautiful residence, which in the
years that followed he filled with a rare collection of works
of art. Here he established a school which was attended by
many pupils.

In 1642 his wife died and he met with financial reverses. His expenditures had exceeded his income and he was deeply in debt. At length he was declared a bankrupt and his valuable collection was sold at public auction, bringing only a small part of what it cost. Because of this misfortune Rembrandt was compelled to pass his last years in poverty, notwithstanding his great ability as an artist.

He is considered a master of light and shade and has been called ''The Prince of Etchers.''

Life, character and above all light were the chief aims of his studies.

If all the lives of Rembrandt were swept out of existence we should still be able to reconstruct his individuality from his pictures. His must have been an intensely emotional nature. . . . The man was tragic in his passionate power. He could not suppress it.—Van Dyke

THE FIGHTING TÉMÉRAIRE

Turner

Now the sunset breezes shiver,
    Téméraire! Téméraire!
And she's fading down the river,
    Téméraire! Téméraire!
Now the sunset breezes shiver,
And she's fading down the river,
But in England's song forever
    She's the Fighting Téméraire.
          —Henry Newbolt, *The Fighting Téméraire*

THE PICTURE

Long and bitter had been the conflict between the two great naval powers of Europe. England on the one hand was proudly proclaiming herself "Mistress of the Seas." France on the other was valiantly struggling to humble that boast.

Now at the close of a decade of battles these nations were floating their navies just off the coast of Trafalgar. Before the close of the day, "Which shall rule the seas?" was to be settled for many years to come. Only a few miles away from the English stronghold the ships of the French navy lay in waiting.

From the top of the English flagship's staff flashed the signal "Move Ahead." The ruddy light of an October day never shown upon a more magnificent spectacle. In perfect unison and manned by the stoutest hearts of England moved the line of ships. Next to the flagship of the commander floated the *Old Téméraire*. To her brave crew was assigned the task of leading the English vessels through the enemy's line.

152

THE FIGHTING TÉMÉRAIRE.—*Turner*

The Battle of Trafalgar is a matter of history. When the news of victory was sent to England the message carried also word of the most gallant ship of the fleet—the *Old Téméraire.* When the disabled vessel, for the *Old Téméraire* had fought her last battle, was towed back to the nation who fondly claimed her, *Old Ironsides* of our own country did not receive a heartier welcome.

Finally it was decided that the *Old Téméraire* should be broken up. It was sunset upon the Thames. The last rays were touching the ripples with that crimson glow which lingers just before the twilight. Nothing disturbed the calm beauty of the scene, save only the gentle motion of a rowboat in which were seated William Turner, the landscape painter, and two friends. Often the oars were rested as they studied the river transfused by the rays of the setting sun.

Suddenly there came across the water the explosive puffs of a steam tug. As it approached nearer and nearer there loomed up gradually behind it the huge proportions of an old-fashioned warship. At close view it appeared in all the tragedy of dismantlement. The sails were idly flapping in the wind and the decks were deserted. There was no sign of life aboard. Snorting and puffing as if gleeful of the ruin it had in tow, the steam tug glided past. That was all. Yet what emotions thrilled the Englishmen.

A huge ship, phantomlike and ghostly, with an odd little vessel puffing in the lead, the distant roofs and spire of the city scarcely discernible through the mist, and the sun at the horizon's brim are the essentials in this interesting subject. With what masterly touches each has been portrayed.

Stripped of all that made her the proudest ship of the English fleet, the *Fighting Téméraire* is slowly moving to the London wharf to be broken up.

Were it possible for wood and iron to possess a soul what emotions might thrill her vast hulk. Yet the sacred memories and associations which cluster about her give as nearly a human individuality to the ship as we could wish. Just such thoughts as these must have inspired the artist to paint her as he did. The old ship was to him a mere semblance of her former self. With amazing tenderness he has enveloped the dismantled frame in a fine mist that broken spars, flapping sails, and deserted decks might not affect us too unpleasantly. In our imagination we are all the more able to go back with him to the halcyon days and exclaim:

> How didst thou trample on tumultuous seas,
> Or, like some basking sea-beast stretched at ease,
>
> .   .   .   .   .
>
> Heroic feet, with fire of genius shod,
> In battle's ecstasy thy deck have trod,
> Now a black beast , belching fire and steam,
> Drags thee away, a pale, dismantled dream.
>
> —Lowell, *Turner's Old Téméraire*

PLAN FOR STUDY

1. **Source of Subject.** The British warship, *Téméraire*, more commonly called *The Fighting Téméraire,* a line-of-battle ship of 98 guns, was captured from the French at the battle of the Nile, 1798. Commanded by Captain Harvey, she fought next to the *Victory* at the Battle of Trafalgar, October 21, 1805.

2. **Setting.** Here we have a sunset scene upon a river. The ghostliness of the larger vessel is emphasized by the gorgeous colors of the sunset. The hour is appropriate for such a subject. The vessel is nearing her end even as the glories of the sunset are fading away. With a noon sunlight over the spectacle, little of the present impressiveness could be felt by the beholder. Observe the effect of the dismantlement of the ship in contributing to the general impression.

3. **Arrangement.** There are two principal ways of arranging the objects in a landscape. One is to place the chief object in the middle of the picture. If this central object is supported on either side by smaller objects, a true triangular arrangement will be effected. The other way is to place the chief object to one side of the canvas with a smaller object on the other side to effect a balance. In this composition, Turner has chosen the latter method, which is conceded by

most critics to be usually the more artistic. The chief object of the composition, the warship with the steam tug, is placed on the left side of the canvas, and it is balanced on the right by a small black spot or buoy.

Can you reason out the advantage this arrangement has over the other form in which the chief objects would be arranged directly in the middle of the composition? A perfect balance is maintained in this canvas, although the single object on the right is so minute. Turner most frequently employs this method of arrangement in his landscape pictures. Can you cite a few examples? Note the effect of the steam tug puffing so energetically in emphasizing the deathlike silence of the larger ship.

From the low horizon line we conclude that the sky is one of the principal motives, if not the chief motive of the artist in this scene. In the distant spires there is only the merest hint of land, while the smokestacks of the tug and the masts of the ship direct our gaze again and again to the sky. Note the means the artist uses in emphasizing the dignity of the warship—by contrast with the small tug, by the vertical lines of the stripped masts and by the unusually "high-set" of the ship in the water. The pathetic touch is shown in the impression of faded glory in the ship.

The line of smoke gives the impression of forward motion. Do you see any evidences of motion in disturbances of the water? The leading vertical lines give the impression of a dignified, measured progress through the water. The horizontal lines of the water and the horizon typify quietude, calm and solemnity. Do you find any suggestion of the diagonal, the line of action? Observe the significance of the men in the rowboat.

We feel the vastness of a scene by the presence of a lone figure. The panoramic grandeur of the sky attracts us the more if it has also appealed to a figure in the picture. . . . When as mere dots men are discerned in a landscape, the vastness of their surroundings is realized at their expense.—Henry Richard Poore

4. **Center of Interest.** The warship is the center of interest. This is emphasized not only by the lighting but it is also

indicated by the title of the picture, the position and size of the vessel, and the general impression given in the setting.

5. **Light and Shade.** If possible secure a good color print of this picture. Turner's greatness lies chiefly in the fine coloring of his pictures. To study a black and white print of Turner is to miss the chief charm of his composition. Note that the glow of the sunset, penetrating to every part of the composition, cementing the objects into one harmonious whole, is the chief unifying agency in the picture. The firmness and dignity of the old warship are further emphasized by the presence of the strongest dark against the object receiving the highest light.

6. **Supreme Idea.** The essential motive of the artist was undoubtedly that of our own Holmes who wrote concerning *Old Ironsides:*

> Ay, tear her tattered ensign down!
> Long has it waved on high,
> And many an eye has danced to see
> That banner in the sky;
> Beneath it rung the battle shout,
> And burst the cannon's roar;—
> The meteor of the ocean air
> Shall sweep the clouds no more!

7. **Color.**

He was very definitely in the habit of indicating the association of any subject with circumstances of death, especially the death of multitudes, by placing it under one of his most deeply crimsoned sunset skies. . . . Subdued by softer hues the color of blood is plainly taken for the leading tone in the storm-clouds above the *Old Téméraire.*

8. **History.** The picture was conceived on the river Thames, 1839, and exhibited the same year. The artist himself loved the picture better than any he had painted. Although fabulous sums were offered for it, he was firm in his decision not to part with it. Upon his death it was found that he had bequeathed it to the English nation, and it now hangs in the National Gallery, London.

COMMENT

Turner is the greatest creator in color, the boldest poet amongst the landscape-painters of all time.—Muther

He was a dreamer of dreams, not a botanist nor an architect, a painter of visions, not a recorder of happenings. He laughed in his sleeve at Ruskin, and, though he sketched as he traveled and knew nature very well, he rather laughed at her also. ''Give me a canvas, colors, a room to work in with a door that will lock, and it is not difficult to paint pictures.'' There the artist speaks. He discarded the actual model and worked from visual memory in the studio. He carried nature in his mind, and painted her out of his head.—Van Dyke

QUESTIONS

What in this scene do you think appealed most to Turner? What method of arrangement did the artist follow in this subject? What points in the setting harmonize with the supreme idea? What is the chief unifying agency? What share of the canvas does the sky occupy? What does this signify? What effect does a vast sky have in a picture? How is balance secured in this composition? What impression is secured by representing the rowboat and its occupants in this scene? How is the dignity and evident worth of the *Téméraire* emphasized? The glories of the sunset are only momentary. Is this in keeping with the real thought of the scene? Why? What is the significance of the red? Of the name *Téméraire?* Were you interested in the history of the old warship? Did it aid you in interpreting the feeling of this subject? How? What impression is given by the vertical lines? The horizontal? The oblique? What are the chief points of beauty in the scene? What were your thoughts in studying the picture? What associations did it call to mind? What insight does the picture give you into the personality of the artist? Does this picture appeal to the eye or to the emotions? What do you think was the motive of the artist in painting this picture? Did he strive to make an accurate copy of the scene, or did he seek only to make the subject interpret his own feelings as he looked upon it? What is the one general impression conveyed by the subject?

THE ARTIST

Turner, Joseph Mallord William (1775—1851), a celebrated English painter, was born in London. His father was a barber. But little is known of his mother. Turner had only a limited education. At the age of twelve he entered the Royal Art Academy and for a brief period he worked with Sir Joshua Reynolds. He first exhibited at the Royal Academy in 1790, and in 1802 he became a member of the faculty there.

Turner was one of the best known landscape painters of all time. His greatness lay chiefly in his originality and coloring. He was a tireless worker for sixty years and exhibited annually in London. He died at Chelsea in 1851. Two rooms in the National Gallery, London, are devoted to his works in oil, and in addition the gallery contains about 300 of his water colors.

The Slave Ship, one of his most celebrated works, is in the Boston Museum of Fine Arts.

His taste was classic. . . . He always idealized his subject, not painting the place itself, but, after having grasped all the principal features of a region, gathering these into one impression, which he placed on paper or canvas.—Hoyt

THE COMING STORM

Inness

Man is permitted much
To scan and learn
In Nature's frame;
Till he well nigh can tame
Brute mischiefs, and can touch
Invisible things, and turn
All warring ills to purposes of good.

—John Henry

Chorus of the Elements

THE PICTURE

What a terrible aspect of nature this scene presents. We seem to be standing afar off on some hilltop and looking out over the peaceful valley and distant moorlands to where the black, threatening clouds presage the storm that is already breaking in all its fury upon the horizon.

From a rift in the lowering mass above us, the sun diffuses its warm glow over meadow and woodland in ghostly contrast to the blackness above and beyond. High in the heavens two great birds soar as though they would outdistance the wind in their wake. Below, with the storm almost upon them, a number of cattle still feed in the sunlit pasture. A lone man chides a couple of loiterers in the valley at our feet.

The elements are at war. Thunder and lightning, rain and wind break upon this summer day with a fury that no human hand can stay. What a magnificent spectacle. We can almost hear the rumble and crash of thunder and see the storm clouds rent again and again with strands of fire. In the distance the trees are bending before the tempest, while nearer the sturdy forest is strangely still in its path.

160

THE COMING STORM.—*Inness*

It is difficult at such a time to picture the quiet aspect of this landscape. Usually—

> Entranced beneath the silent, moving sky,
>   The long, green meadows move without a sound;
> A breeze soft passes with a butterfly,
>   A lonely hawk soars low above the ground—
> The thin cloud-shadows drift upon their noiseless round.
>
> —Douglas Roberts

Changed indeed is that serene spirit. Sunshine is giving way to the blackness of a pall, summer zephyrs to the violence of a gale. But nature's children are not dismayed, and herein lies a certain comforting truth.

The sturdy trees that just now nod wisely and prepare for the strain of storm-swept branches have withstood for years the attacks of just such warring elements. The birds, so happy and tuneful the livelong day, are strangely hushed, it is true, but they are not afraid. The cows may be forced to seek shelter, but an instinct within promises a speedy return of the calmness of the June day which now rests over the pasture. Even this man, alone and away from home, is not hopeless in the face of the coming storm. He, too, from experience has learned of the goodness of a Providence who decrees that fair days shall succeed stormy ones.

> . . . But not for aye can last
> The storm, and sweet the sunshine when 'tis past.
> Lo, the clouds roll away—they break,—they fly,
> And, like the glorious light of summer, cast
> O'er the wide landscape from the embracing sky,
> On all the peaceful world the smile of heaven shall lie.
>
> —Bryant, *After a Tempest*

PLAN FOR STUDY

1. **Source of Subject.** To Inness has been given the credit of discovering the American landscape. Since most of his painting was done in the state of New York, he evidently found there all the material necessary for the great number of landscapes which bear his signature. The scene of this picture

represents a typical New York valley and woodland. He made several preliminary studies for this painting, one small one with the same title and dated 1865 being especially well done. A few years before his death he painted still another of the same subject, which he kept.

The position of Inness in American painting is analogous to that held in French painting by the Barbizon masters. Both schools broke away from the classic landscape; both represented with truth the familiar landscape about them. Inness might well be said to have done pioneer work in American landscape painting. Few, if any, of his contemporaries in America appreciated the possibilities of the landscape which could be seen just outside their own windows. A subject for a great picture to their minds must represent some scene far removed, say in classic Italy or Greece. Inness from boyhood loved the familiar landscape. Within a small area he found subjects which it took a lifelong devotion to his art to represent truthfully and artistically.

Just as the Barbizon school brought the people of France to appreciate the beauty of common things, so did Inness in America discover to his countrymen the hidden beauties of their own land. He loved to paint all phases of the atmosphere, all seasons, and all the various moods of nature. He especially delighted in representing vast areas with infinite stretches of sky. He delighted, too, in storm effect, but could just as effectively paint nature in her softest moods.

2. **Setting.** First, observe the details that suggest the approaching storm—the flight of the birds, the swaying branches of the trees in the distance, the activity of the man in the foreground, the low horizon line suggesting that the motive of the scene is in the sky itself. Observe the effect of the contrast between the sunny pasture and the blackness overhead and beyond. Note the glimpse of several human habitations and the effect. Consider the vastness of the scene, and notice how this is emphasized by the lone figure of the man. The observer is looking down upon the landscape from a lofty elevation, and the view is typical of many scenes among the Adirondacks and Catskills. It is safe to presume that the

original sketch for the picture was made from one of the mountains in New York. The effect of the scene would be lost if it were viewed from the plain in the foreground.

3. **Arrangement.** We have noted in the setting the unusual viewpoint from which we look upon the spectacle. Here we have a very good example of synthetic treatment, that is to say, a general omission of detail resulting in a grand mustering of all the elements to give the impression of the approaching tempest. How briefly the interest is held in the lower plane. Mere brush strokes serve to represent the trees of the background, while those at the right and in the foreground are painted in comparative detail. See how the suggestion of houses in the different planes serves to measure the broad extent of the landscape. Observe with what skill the storm is represented as breaking upon the horizon, the characteristic calm which precedes it in the motionless foliage of the trees in the foreground, and the majesty with which the gathering storm clouds clothe the sky. Study the examples of balance in the arrangement.

4. **Center of Interest.** The title, the subordination of all land objects, and the space occupied by the sky lead us to the immediate conclusion that the motive is in the sky itself, where there is every evidence of an approaching storm. The eye centers instantly upon the black clouds on the horizon.

5. **Supreme Motive.** It is not difficult to understand the motive or appreciate the emotions of the artist who renders nature here in this intensely dramatic aspect. The contemplation of a storm brings to all much the same emotion—a feeling of awe in the presence of the infinite. Inness, who was by nature deeply religious, probably experienced this emotion to a greater degree than most of us. He said:

The true purpose of the painter is simply to reproduce in other minds the impression which a scene has made upon him. A work of art does not appeal to the intellect. It does not appeal to the moral sense. Its aim is not to instruct, not to edify, but to awaken an emotion. This emotion may be one of love, of pity, of veneration, of hate, of pleasure or of pain; but it must be a single emotion, if the work has unity, as every such work should have, and the true beauty of the work consists in the beauty of the sentiment or emotion which it inspires. . . . Rivers, streams, the rippling brook, the hillside, the sky, clouds,—all things that we see—can convey that sentiment if we are in love of God and the desire of truth. Some persons suppose that the landscape has no power of conveying human sentiment. But this is a great mistake. The civilized landscape peculiarly can, and therefore I love it and think it more worthy of reproduction than that which is savage and untamed. It is more significant.

Inness painted what his heart inspired him to paint without much regard to the subject of his picture. If he looked upon a landscape it was the impression that it made upon his own mind that he desired to paint upon his canvas. He did not aim to reproduce a scene with accuracy, he left that for the camera to do. Coxe relates a story that nicely brings out this characteristic of the painter. Once after selling a picture in his studio, the purchaser asked,

"Now, Mr. Inness, where is that taken from; what part of the country?"

"Nowhere in particular; do you suppose I illustrate guide-books? That's a picture."

6. **Light and Shade.** Study the lighting after the plan followed in other landscape subjects.

7. **History.** This picture, signed G. Inness and dated 1878, was purchased in 1900 by the Buffalo Academy of Fine Arts with the income from the Albert Haller Tracy Fund. It is twenty-five and one-fourth inches high by thirty-eight and one-fourth inches wide.

QUESTIONS

What are your feelings as you study this picture? From where do you seem to be looking? What signs do you see of the coming storm? What is the general character of the country? What is the expression of nature in this scene? How is distance shown? How are the different trees represented? Can you see the man and cattle plainly? Why not? Is this true to nature? Do you suppose the artist wished us to be much interested in them? Why does he represent them here at all? What would be the effect if they were left out? What did he wish us to study most in the scene? Why do you say this? How much of the picture is occupied by the sky? What does this tell us about the artist's motive? What colors would you use in coloring the picture? What sounds do you seem to hear? What movements do you seem to see? What one truth is the artist trying to give us in the subject? What were his thoughts, do you suppose, as he represented this scene? What are the beautiful qualities of the landscape? What suggestion does the view of the homes bring? What do you like most about the scene? Where is the center of interest? What season of the year is represented? How does the artist show this? What is the time of day? Why do you think so?

THE ARTIST

Inn'ess, George (1825—1894), an American landscape painter, was born at Newburg, N. Y. At the age of fourteen years he was apprenticed to an engraver. He received some instruction in drawing and in 1843 began a close study of nature. The same year he entered the studio of Regis Gignoux. After this he traveled and studied in France and Italy at three different periods. In 1862 Inness located in New Jersey and in 1868 he was elected national academician. He died at Bridge of Allan, Scotland, in 1894. The same year an extensive exhibition of his works was held in the Fine Arts Building, New York City. His pictures are in all the leading galleries of the United States and Europe. *Under the Greenwood, Autumn Gold, Close of a Stormy Day, Pine Groves of Barberini Villa,* and *Tenafly Oaks* are among his most celebrated works.

It was with color, light, and air that Inness scored his greatest success. —Van Dyke

His aim is always pure, and his inspiration is always felt.—Sheldon

A pathfinder whose original and fiery zeal for nature blazed a new trail that has led on to the present notable expansion of American landscape painting.—Caffin

> He might be called the preacher painter, finding
> Tongues in trees, books in running brooks,
> Sermons in stones and good in everything.
>   —McSpadden

SEPTEMBER

Zuber

The groves were God's first temples, ere man learned
To hew the shaft, and lay the architrave,
And spread the roof above them—ere he framed
The lofty vault, to gather and roll back
The sound of anthems.
Here is continual worship;—Nature, here,
In the tranquillity that thou dost love,
Enjoys thy presence.

—Bryant, *A Forest Hymn*

THE PICTURE

Come, we go today to the fields and woods. September skies are over us. September glories are all about us. Along the roadside where the goldenrod stretches in a never-ending margin, through fields of ripening corn, and meadows of flower and stubble, our path leads us to the cool, September woods. Here we come to a spot of the poet's own choosing. Giant oaks tower above us on every hand, spreading a canopy of nature's green.

Here in the shade we linger while September harmonies fill our souls. Here, too, these patient cows have come from the sunlit meadow yonder, and just beyond this tree at our left some campers are resting.

Shall we let Nature be our teacher? With eyes open to the glories about us, let us stand perfectly quiet for a moment. See these trees, their gnarled branches so lavishly bedecked with leaves. What a lesson of faith, of aspiration, of generous sharing they teach us. Centuries ago, a tiny acorn fell in the spot where each now stands. It responded heartily to the gentle rains and soil and sun, and it sprang to a soul in a tiny

167

shoot. Nature became the tenderest of gardeners and spread about it the purest environment. Years passed. The shoot became at last the sturdy oak, now crowned with the beauty and experience of ripe old age. What an asset is such a tree to any forest. Undaunted, it weathers the winter's gales to be crowned in the spring, year after year, with a wealth of foliage. How unselfishly it shares the charms Nature has given it. In its branches the birds flit to and fro and build their homes. In the cool shade beneath, Nature's children rest and thank the Giver who blessed the earth with trees.

A song to the oak, the brave old oak,
  Who hath stood in the greenwood long;
Here's health and renown to his broad green crown,
  And his fifty arms so strong.
There's fear in his frown when the sun goes down,
  And the fire in the west fades out;
And he showeth his might on a wild midnight,
  When the storms through the branches shout.

—Henry Fothergill Chorley, *The Brave Old Oak*

But how soon the woodman's ax can destroy what nature has been centuries in bringing to maturity. A few hours' work and the "brave old oak" lies prostrate on the ground, its trunk to be made into lumber or used for fuel and its branches probably burned in a brush heap. Trees are for use as well as for ornament, but many are destroyed without cause, and the welfare of the country is being seriously impaired by the ruthless destruction of forests. Let us resolve, as we study this picture, that we will never consent to the felling of a tree unless it is a positive necessity.

What a joy there is in the air we breathe. The hot, sultry summer days are gone. September winds stir the clear, bracing atmosphere, and waft along the fresh odors of the September woods.

All Nature is at peace. It is as if she were resting from her efforts in the growing season. Crops are soon to be gathered—golden corn of the fields, russet apples of the orchards, purple grapes of the vineyards.

SEPTEMBER.—*Zuber*

What a vista greets our eye just beyond the trees. Can you not hear the call of the fields? Listen:

There's a haze that hides the meadows and the river from the hills;
There's a wealth of royal purple where the cricket chirps and trills;
There is gold in rich abundance—come and gather while ye may;
Come and breathe the breath of summer—gain a lifetime in a day.

For the sumach bush is all aflame, the maple catches fire;
From twig to twig the color runs as high the flames aspire.
Come and breathe the breath of summer—there's a whisper in the trees
That she's going, going, going. Who would lose such days as these?

—Virginia Lewis

PLAN FOR STUDY

The landscape has been fully treated in *The Haymakers, The Balloon,* and *The Coming Storm.* Use these plans in the study of this picture.

September was painted in 1885.

QUESTIONS

What season of the year is represented in this picture? What time of day do you think it is? Why? What is the picture about? How many cows do you see? What are they doing? Are they all doing the same thing? How many parts to this picture? (Two, field and woods.) In which are you most interested? Why? Do you see any evidence of people in the picture? What are they doing, do you suppose? Have you ever been in a woods like this on a September day? What did you see? What colors did you note? What sounds? What odors? What kind of trees are these? How do you know? Do you admire this type of tree? What do you like most about it? Where is the highest light? Do you see any shadows that might tell you from what direction the light comes? How does the light enter the woods? What serves to bring out the lacy effect of the branches? Did you ever plant a tree? What good does a tree do? Do you think the title of this picture a good one? Can you suggest a better one? **Try.**

Where does your eye linger longest in the picture? Why can you not see the cows farthest away more plainly? Do you think the artist loved nature and natural scenes? What is he trying to tell you in this picture? Does he tell it plainly?

> Sweet is the voice that calls
> From babbling water-falls
> In meadows where the downy seeds are flying;
> And soft the breezes blow,
> And eddying come and go
> In faded gardens where the rose is dying.
>
> —George Arnold

THE ARTIST

Zuber, Jean Henri (1844——), a landscape artist, was born in Rexheim, Alsace. He was a pupil of Gleyre, from whom he learned much. In 1875 he was awarded third- and second-class medals, and in 1886 he was elected a member of the Legion of Honor. Some of his other works of note are, *Bad Weather*, *The Lost Path*, *After the Harvest*. He is represented in the Luxembourg Gallery.

THE LAKE

Corot

Over head the tree-tops meet,
Flowers and grass spring 'neath one's feet;
There was naught above me, naught below,
My childhood had not learned to know:
For what are the voices of birds—
Ay, and of beasts,—but words, our words,
Only so much more sweet.

—Browning

THE PICTURE

Tender saplings and trees with mountain-like tops of soft feathery foliage massed against the sky, and a broad smooth lake extending to the distant hills make up the setting. It is as if storms had never ruffled the calm surface of the lake or tossed the branches of the trees. Even the cows are attracted by the restfulness of the place. Here in the cool shallow waters they are standing quite content.

To the left, a little arm of water reaches into the foreground. On its bank an old herdsman holding his strong staff is resting in keeping with the spirit of the place.

The sun shines full upon the lake, while here and there the rays pierce the deep shadows of the glade. The whole scene breathes the freshness of the morning, the hour the artist best loved to paint. He wrote of such a time,

It is charming, the day of the landscapist. One rises early at three o'clock in the morning before the sun shines. He does not see much at first—everything is scented, everything trembles with the fresh breeze of dawn.

Bing! the sun is clear, it has not yet torn away the mist behind which are hidden the hills of the horizon. Bing! Bing! a first ray of the sun, a second ray of the sun. The little flowers seem to awake joyously. The leaves shiver in the morning breeze. In the trees the invisible birds are chirping. It seems to be the flowers offering up their prayers.

172

THE LAKE.—*Corot*

Bam! Bam! the sun has risen. Everything glistens, everything is brilliant, everything is in full purple light. The flowers hold up their heads, the birds fly hither and thither. The mist rises and reveals the lake plated with silver and nature in masses fresh and fragrant.

How happy must be the artist to whom the dawn of day breathes such an impression. We may be sure the glories of his favorite hour have touched this scene. In the branches the birds are surely singing. Dotting the margin of the water, the wild flowers are lifting their heads.

In the strong old figure clad in coarse peasant garb there seems some of the tranquillity of the hour. Such perfect peace and rest kings do not enjoy. Should we condole with him the loneliness of such a life we may be sure he would answer in the spirit of the Duke of Arden:

> Hath not old custom made this life more sweet
> Than that of painted pomp, are not these woods
> More free from peril than the court?

What graceful, tremulous trees! The leaning tree to the left with its scanty branches stands out in strong contrast with the dense foliage of the larger ones. How gracefully the foliage seems to sway in the gentle breeze.

Here upon the margin of the lake the bushes and tall branches bend over the water. Bright splashes of light touch the dark foliage. Having once seen these trees we shall always be able to identify a landscape by Corot. Only the graceful types—the aspen, the willow or the poplar appealed to him. He delighted to paint them with a feathery foliage that floats in every gale.

True to the principle with which the camera plate blurs a moving surface, the artist suggests motion in the blurred foliage of the branches. We seem to see the leaves stir even as the light patches lengthen and shorten in unison.

A multitude of details have been so carefully subordinated that our eyes take in the whole at a glance. The two trees in the foreground serve to concentrate the most important lines of the setting. Note how the leaning tree follows the triangular form of the foliage. The green grass and shadowy margin of the water, the soft gray trunks and the foliage massed against the bright glow of the sky, enhance the setting with a coloring delicate and in harmony with the spirit.

The key to Corot's motive in landscape painting as he expresses it is:

Place yourself face to face with nature and seek to render it with pre· cision; paint what you see and interpret the impression received.

If thou art worn and hard beset
With sorrows, that thou wouldst forget
If thou wouldst read a lesson, that will keep
Thy heart from fainting and thy soul from sleep,
Go to the woods and hills. No tears
Dim the sweet look that Nature wears.

—Longfellow, *Sunrise on the Hills*

PLAN FOR STUDY

The landscape has been generally treated in subjects of Ruysdael, Inness, Troyon and others. Refer to those studies for a method of treatment of this picture.

COMMENT

Corot enchanted me. There was a silvery pool of his that reflected back the sky and the trees wet with the morning dew that recalled to my mind hours spent in childhood wandering along borders of the ponds in our carperie.—Jules Breton

Landscapes are refined suggestions, delineating rather the impression made by scenery on a poetic mind than the facts of scenery; his representation of trees is the best possible definition of tree-painting as an art, distinguished from tree-drawing in botany.—National Magazine

Indeed, so many landscapes are full of the suggestion of poetry, and we speak of them as poetic landscapes. This does not mean that they illustrate any particular poem, but that they affect one's imagination in somewhat the same way as poetry does. The reason is that such artists have the spirits of poets.—Caffin

QUESTIONS

What is the nature of the setting? What general arrangement has the artist here observed? What is the impression given by the setting? What are the component parts that give it? What is the impression of the herdsman's figure? What are the distinctive characteristics of the trees? Compare this setting with that of *Joan of Arc*. What is the essential difference? Which is the most pleasing? In which was the painter working to represent mere visible appearance? In which was he endeavoring to interpret his own feelings? Does this landscape appeal to the eye or to the feelings? What feelings are inspired by it? Where is the center of interest? How has the artist dealt with mere details? To what has he subordinated them? What are the beautiful as well as the interesting features of the landscape? What trait of the artist's character is here indicated?

THE ARTIST

Corot, *Ko rō'*, **Jean Baptiste Camille** (1796—1875), a French landscape painter, was born at Paris, 1796. He was a pupil of Michallon and Bertin. He first exhibited at the Salon of 1827. He studied in Italy, Spain and England, and opened his studio in Paris. The Legion of Honor medal was conferred on him, 1846.

Few men were more successful or more beloved than Corot— few were so happy, so pure, so generous. Petty trivialities never troubled him. Of a great master he modestly exclaimed, "I am only a lark, I sing my little songs in my clouds, he is like the eagle soaring in the heavens." He was a leader in the famous Fontainebleau-Barbizon School, a school of landscape painters devoted to the naturalistic style of landscape. Among these were Dupre, Millet, Rousseau and Diaz. They found inspiration in the old Dutch masterpieces in the Louvre, and an incentive to study the natural landscape right at their door. The forest of Fontainebleau and the fields of Barbizon became their resort. Their landscapes are notable for their lighting, color, and above all for the impression they give.

Other pictures: *Dance of the Nymphs,* 1851; *Orpheus Greeting the Morn.*

Corot's temperament was classic in the true sense; trembling to the subtlest suggestion of nature, but also governed by a delicate sense of poise, harmony and rhythm.—Caffin

In his landscape he suppresses all but the significant and gives the constant features, those upon which nature works her changes, and, therefore, presents her ever ready for change, in indecision, "on the wing."—Stranahan

What, for instance, is more apparent than the charm of Corot as seen in his landscapes? His pictures delight us by their alluring qualities of calmness, radiance, unity. They are fair dreams of splendor in which dawn and twilight glow through a silver veil of atmosphere, in which the winds are hushed and the waters are stilled and that peace which passeth understanding, that joy which is beyond price have fallen upon the dwellers in Arcadia.—Van Dyke

THE AURORA

Guido Reni

Day!
Faster and more fast,
O'er night's brim, day boils at last;
Boils, pure gold, o'er the cloud-cups brim.
Where spurting and supprest it lay,
For not a froth-flake touched the brim
Of yonder gap in the solid gray
Of the eastern cloud, an hour away;
But forth one wavelet, then another, curled,
Till the whole sunrise, not to be supprest,
Rose, reddened, and its seething breast
Flickered in bounds, grew gold, then overflowed the world.

—Browning, *Day Break*, from *Pippa Passes*

THE PICTURE

Where are the palaces of the gods? How may we find the
rosy path leading to the thrones whereon immortal beings
decree the seasons of rain and sunshine, of bitter blasts and
balmy June days, of seed time and bountiful golden harvests?

We might inquire of the astronomers and the wisest doctors
or of the most learned philosophers and they would not know.
The gifted fairies cannot tell us, nor does the rainbow lead
to it. But this land does exist and immortal beings do reign!

Far, far in the east above the clouds and above the highest
mountain peaks are the glittering domes and golden walls of
their castles. There in the grandest of the palaces, on a throne
of gold, thickly inlaid with costly jewels, reigns the mighty
god of day.

The whole world rejoiced when he took up the sceptre. It
is said that the sunbeams in their delight danced on the waves;
"that singing swans flew seven times around the island of
Delos."

THE AURORA.—*Guido Reni*

Near by, his beautiful sister Diana, gentle goddess of the night, reigns in a throne-room of ivory and gold. But it is his other sister, rosy Aurora, the goddess of dawn, who ministers most to him. Her daily duties are always the same. Every morning she awakens her brother and accompanies him in his race across the heavens.

Few in all the kingdom are more beloved than Aurora. Loveliest of all the goddesses, she is the white-robed messenger of light, joy, peace and "giver of all good things." The stars, the morning and evening breezes are her children.

But what is this change that has come over the kingdom? Diana, the beautiful queen of night, putting out the stars and gathering up the moonbeams, is hurrying through the blue mist of the sky. Bright-eyed Cupids with flaring torches lead the way. Now suddenly a bright light glorifies the place.

Aurora in flowing draperies rushes out of her palace. Hurrying to the palace of the god of day, she raps at the window of his sleeping room. At her touch the doors of the palace fly open and the Hours come dancing forth. The silver bars of the royal stables fall away as if by magic and out rush the prancing steeds, pawing the earth impatiently with their golden hoofs. Quickly the Hours harness them to the golden chariot. A quick jerk of the reins, a burst of song, and up and away fly the merry host.

Out into the morning clouds, over the spires and walls of countless cities they rush. In their path the darkness is shattered by shafts of sunshine radiating from the sun-god's chariot. Onward and ever upward they press while the morning breezes follow in their wake and waft the rose-tinted clouds along.

Birds awake and fill the air with their merry song. Dew-sprinkled flowers sway in the gentle breezes. The whole eastern sky is aflame with the light, and soft clouds roll crimson, then gold, then silver. Far below, the people open their eyes to the new day.

Now the heavenly beings are high in the heavens and the morning breezes droop and fall behind. Down the western slope the sun-god urges the flying steeds. Far in the west the goddess of night awaits their coming. The chariot rushes past. For only a moment is its path outlined in the crimson glory of sky and earth and then it disappears below the horizon. The day is done.

The world has long since ceased to believe in the land of gods or in this chariot journey across the sky. But this fine old myth has never lost its charm and we delight to hear it even to this day. Poets and painters have been thrilled with the beauty of its spirit. So that when a citizen of Rome ordered a fresco for his garden pavilion, the artist chose for its subject this journey of the sun-god.

A glorious host—dancing, sparkling, joyous maidens, a sun-god's lordly figure, madly prancing snow-white steeds, rosy Cupid with flaming torch and the radiant goddess of morn—all sweep past on lofty clouds that float grandly, swiftly onward—one splendid spectacle of motion and color—a morning poem of the heavens! What grace! What magnificent coloring! It is as if the artist had filled his brush with the crimson, purple and gold of the rainbow, brightened with the fresh tints of the sunrise.

Phoebus Apollo, handsome, graceful creator of all this splendor, rides his golden chariot in its midst. With what skill the artist represented him. We are made to feel his power in those calm but resolute features, in that powerful hand directing with ease the coursers. Clustering curls add to the youthful beauty of a well-poised head. Muscles of chest and neck grow tense as he bends before the upward charge of his horses. Ever onward, ever upward he glides while just ahead golden-haired Cupid heralds his approach.

And what shall we say of these beautiful maidens dancing about his chariot? Grand and lordly he seems in their midst. They are the Hours who must accompany him. Hand in hand they move with sweeping draperies along the golden path. Their flying feet seem scarcely to touch the clouds while their joyous spirits find expression in tuneful snatches of song.

As if anxious to share her own enthusiasm with them, the gayest, airiest of the Hours points ahead to the dawn. What varied expressions their faces show. These three Hours gliding along so gracefully in the full morning light are the merriest, most youthful of the group. Their blithe spirits seem the fount of all the freshness and beauty of the morning hour.

Their sisters, however, on the other side do not seem to share in the general happiness. They are the afternoon Hours, and, conscious of the declining day, are sadly completing their round of time. Above them little Cupid is borne rapidly along. Innocent, rosy morning-star is he, and he performs his task right well.

But if the onward rush of the Hours is graceful and spirited, how must we describe the furious speed of the horses? With flowing manes and forms so airy yet powerful, they seem to spurn the clouds and dash "up a hill perpendicular". So rapid is their progress it is hard to tell whether they are flying or leaping. Together they move with rapid, even pace, drawing the chariot in triumphant flight.

Yet it is for the goddess of morn floating so gracefully ahead that the dew laden flowers of fields and valleys are lifting their heads. Fresh balmy breezes stir at her approach. Truly

> Aurora doth with gold adorn
> The ever beauteous eyelids of the morn

Best loved of the deities, she alone can usher in the day. Darkness melts before the gold-tinted cloud on which she floats, while at her approach the stars hasten to close their eyes.

Far beneath, the fields, woodlands and cities are stirring from their slumber. The horizon has caught the glow of the sunrise and is sharing it with the deep blue of the sea. Everywhere the earth, fresh and pure, glistens in the morning light.

Where are the palaces of the gods? Is it true that they do exist? We make haste to answer, no! But have we not often marveled, as did the Greeks and Romans of old, at the mystery of the sunrise? Have we not seen Apollo's arrows of gleaming gold leap from mountain cliff and crag and pierce the soft, crimson clouds of the eastern sky? Then as we watched did not the whole heavens blaze in splendor, and all earth wax radiant? And did not our thoughts become as fresh and pure as the morning all about us?

If in our study of this masterpiece we are uplifted with these same lofty sentiments we shall have read aright the conception of the artist. Then only shall we share with thousands our own rightful inheritance of a true appreciation of the *Aurora*.

PLAN FOR STUDY

1. **Source of the Subject.** The source of the artist's conception is to be found in Greek and Roman mythology. Aurora, the goddess of the dawn (called Eos by the Greeks), Helios (in later times identified with Phoebus Apollo), the sun-god, and Lucifer (identified with Cupid), together with the Hours, are the chief actors in this spectacle. There is a distinction, however, between Phoebus Apollo, the son of Zeus, representing the light-giving and life-giving influences as well as the deadly power of the sun, and Helios, the sun-god, son of Hyperion and Titaness Theia. It is Helios, strong, beautiful and impetuous, who drives the four-horse chariot. However, the driver of the horses in Guido Reni's painting is almost universally called Phoebus Apollo. While strictly speaking this is not true, the identifying of the one with the other has become quite customary, and we have followed the custom in our description of the painting.

2. **Setting.** A heaven-born company here traverse the clouds. In their divine origin earth's gravitation has no effect upon them. They impress us as even spurning this aerial pathway. There is no limit to the heights they may go. As a decorative effect, the painting has never been surpassed. Observe, then, everything in the setting that contributes to its decorative qualities. Brilliance, airiness, great hurrying power, ecstasy, tunefulness and concord are a few of the components of the single dominating impression. Find others. Note how the idea of loftiness is intensified by the view of the fields and mountains far below. In the distance the sea gives depth to the horizon.

3. **Arrangement.** If we bear in mind that the supreme purpose of the painting was a decorative one, its chief defect will

not appear so glaring. Critics are quite generally agreed that
the composition lacks unity. The conception is a noble one,
the sweep of these beautiful creatures across the heavens leaves
an impression that will linger long in the mind. But it is well
for us to understand in just what respect the picture fails of
meeting the supreme test of a work of art. Here we have five
features that appeal to the eye with varying degrees of intensity, namely: Aurora, Apollo, Lucifer, the horses, the Hours.
Perfect unity of all the parts of the picture requires that there
be but one center of interest. This necessitates subordination
of all other parts, and this may be accomplished by the lighting,
by the position and size of the central object, by the leading
lines, mental and physical, or by a combination of all these, but
chiefly by the strength of the central figure. Where is the
center of interest here? Are we quite sure that it is Apollo,
or is it not Aurora?

There is a multiplicity of details in the composition whose
tendency is to confuse the eye. It is imperative, then, that a
central feature dominate the picture if a single impression is
to be given. Do we find that the figure in the chariot is strong
enough to rule every other feature, or is our interest not
divided with Aurora, a little in the lead? It is in this respect
that most critics are inclined to say that the sun-god here is
somewhat disappointing.

Yet as a decorative scheme the fresco is not surpassed. Its
vitality is marvelous. Observe the effect of the flying draperies, entwining arms and flying feet of the Hours, the whirling chariot wheels, the sweep of Apollo's mantle, the backward trend of Cupid's fire, the flowing manes and upward
dash of the horses in conveying the impression of rapid motion.
Does not the circular arrangement of the Hours suggest the
clock?

4. Central Point of Interest. Apollo in his chariot is designed
to be the center of interest. As noted in the arrangement,
however, the central figure here is not strong enough to rule
every other point of interest in the scene. In this respect the
composition fails to meet perfectly the supreme test—a singleness and a definiteness of impression.

5. Color.

The color is vivid and brilliant, though the blue, both of the sky and sea, is rather cold and hard.—Hillard

The picture is as fresh and brilliant as if he had painted it with the morning sunshine which it represents. It could not be more lustrous in its hues, if he had given it the last touch an hour ago.—Hawthorne

6. **History.** Cardinal Scipio Borghese, in 1604, commissioned Guido Reni to fresco the Casino of his Palace on the Quirinal, built in 1603 and located on the site of the Baths of Constantine. The Casino, or garden pavilion, delightfully situated at the end of a garden planted with magnolias, consists of three halls on the ground floor. On the ceiling of the central hall is the *Aurora*. A large mirror has been placed below in such a way as to enable the visitor to view the fresco in comfort. After the Cardinal's death the Palace became the abode of the French ambassadors until 1704, when it passed to the Rospigliosi family. The present owners very graciously open the Casino to the public on certain days of the week.

The Aurora is listed with the twelve great pictures of the world.

COMMENT

The alacrity and movement, morning stir and glow of the picture are wonderful. It seems impossible to catch its glory in a copy. . . . My memory, I believe, will be somewhat enlivened by this picture hereafter: not that I remember it very distinctly even now; but bright things leave a sheen and glimmer in the mind, like Christian's tremulous glimpse of the Celestial City.—Hawthorne

This is the noblest work of Guido. It is embodied poetry. . . . Nothing is more admirable in this beautiful composition than the motion given to the whole.—Eaton

Guido's ''*Aurora*'' is the very type of haste and impetus; for surely no man ever imagined such hurry and tumult, such sounding and clashing.—Mendelssohn's Letters

QUESTIONS

What is the dominant impression? What does the picture represent? It is generally conceded to be one of the finest decorative pieces in the world. What are the qualities that give it such a claim? Where is the center of interest? How is it emphasized? Comment upon the comparative strengths of the figures of the sun-god and Aurora as chief objects of interest. What do the Hours typify? What qualities do they contribute to the scene as a whole? What is the significance of the sun-god? Aurora? Cupid? What is the impression given by the setting? How is the impression of motion given? What are the most attractive features? What emotions are awakened? What impression is likely to be the most lasting one? Does the conception indicate anything as to the character of the painter? What, for example? With what do you think he was most concerned, the decorative effect that he would produce or some emotion of his own that he wished his subject to reflect?

THE ARTIST

Reni, Guido, *Rā'nē Gwē'dō* (1575—1642), a celebrated Italian painter, was born at Calvenzano, near Bologna.

There was a time when for three hundred years Italy produced the greatest artists the world has ever known. Some of these masters we have already studied. With the death of Michelangelo, the glorious period began to wane. It was then that Guido Reni was born in Bologna.

When a boy he had put aside his love for music that he might study painting. So rapidly did he master the essentials that at thirteen years he was allowed to teach other pupils.

He studied with Calvart and Caracci, but early went to Rome, where he spent the greater part of his life.

At first his works seemed full of promise, especially when he reached the heights in his *Aurora*. Towards the end, however, his work, being carelessly and too hastily done, degenerated. His paintings may be classed as mythological, historical and portraiture. Grace, rhythm and beauty are characteristic of the best of them.

His other pictures of note are, *Massacre of the Innocents*, at Bologna; *The Assumption of the Virgin*, Vatican; *Beatrice Cenci*, Rome; and *Crucifixion of St. Peter*, Vatican

HOLY NIGHT

Correreggio

His birth-bed shall be neither
In housen nor in hall,
Nor in the place of paradise,
But in the oxen's stall.

He neither shall be rockèd
In silver nor in gold,
But in the wooden manger
That lieth in the mould.

—*Christmas Carol*

THE PICTURE

All day long multitudes thronged the streets of Bethlehem. Throughout all Judea had gone forth the summons that all inhabitants meet in their own cities to be taxed. The order of the ruler must be obeyed, and from far and near the people journeyed to the cities. From the region of Galilee Joseph and Mary had come, the message having reached them as Joseph plied his trade in the shop. All the houses were crowded, and Joseph inquired for shelter again and again, only to hear the oft repeated "no room at the inn". At the close of day they came upon an old shed just outside the village.

And there were in the same country shepherds abiding in the field, keeping watch over their flock by night. And, lo, the angel of the Lord came upon them, and the glory of the Lord shone round about them: and they were sore afraid. And the angel said unto them, Fear not: for, behold, I bring you good tidings of great joy, which shall be to all people. For unto you is born this day in the city of David a Saviour, which is Christ the Lord. And this shall be a sign unto you; Ye shall find the babe wrapped in swaddling clothes, lying in a manger. And suddenly there was with the angel a multitude of the heavenly host praising God, and saying, Glory to God in the highest, and on earth peace, good will toward men.—Luke II:8-14.

The stars above took part on that joyous night, flooding the plain with a lustrous glow. While the shepherds debated among themselves concerning the wonderful message, choirs of angels filled earth and sky with their joyful music. With songs of praise the shepherds hurried across the hills to Bethlehem. There the glorious music of the angel choir ushered them into the place where, "wrapped in swaddling clothes," they found the Christ-Child.

It is the light—pure white, radiant, brilliant—that transfigures the humble scene, shines full upon the face of the fond mother, dazzles the shepherds, illumines the angelic host and fills the cave with a heavenly glow. Even the commonplace wheat straws become threads of gold in its path. The mother kneeling before the wooden manger is unaffected by the light which shines full upon her happy face. Very different, however, is the effect upon the shepherdess near by. Desiring to look steadily at the Saviour, she is unable to do so. One hand must screen her eyes. In the other she holds a little basket containing a present of turtle doves.

At her side stand the shepherds. How strong they look. The weakness of the tiny babe and the gentleness of the mother are strongly emphasized when contrasted with these sturdy men. The younger man, one arm resting on the manger and the other caressing the dog, is regarding the hovering angels with rapt attention. The strong old herdsman at his side seems bewildered with the scene and has raised his hand to his head as he stands awed before the Christ. The great staff which has aided him in his journey over the hills is grasped in his powerful left hand.

Lending joy and beauty to the scene, the heavenly host float on the clouds above. How joyful must be the song of these angels hovering so lightly that they seem "showered down from heaven." Through the doorway the gray light of the dawn bathing the eastern sky is seen behind the distant mountains. It seems cold and earthly indeed as it approaches the light which fills the cave.

Centuries have passed since the execution of this picture and time has marred its delicate tones. Yet in its radiant

HOLY NIGHT.—*Correggio*

glow we can still read the story of that wonderful scene in Bethlehem.

> It is the calm and silent night!
>   A thousand bells ring out, and throw
> Their joyous peals abroad, and smite
>   The darkness—charmed and holy now!
> The night that erst no shame had worn,
>   To it a happy name is given;
> For in that stable lay, new-born,
>   The peaceful Prince of earth and heaven,
> In the solemn midnight,
>   Centuries ago!
>
> —Alfred Domett, *Christian Hymn*

PLAN FOR STUDY

1. **Source of Subject.** The Saviour's birth as told by St. Luke. The artist, however, was not quite satisfied with the mere suggestion of a setting in the story, but was led to paint the charming setting of this picture by the account given in the apocryphal gospels which describe the Christ-Child "shining with a brilliant light" and the cave as "filled with light more beautiful than the glittering lamps and candles brighter than the light of the sun."

2. **Setting.** St. Luke tells us that Christ was born in a stable. The birthplace as described in the apocryphal gospels was a cave. Correggio chose to differ from both these authorities. Accordingly he selected as the scene of the picture an old shed supported by the ruins of an edifice, the steps and columns of which are still standing. The presence of the shepherds and the animals add much to the human interest of the scene. The angel choir and the glory of the supernatural light give to the picture a heavenly atmosphere in which, strangely enough, these humble folk of the plains have a place in perfect harmony with the supreme idea. Then, too, the father, busy in the doorway, suggests the activity of the great, real world just outside.

Thus in all the celestial glory of the scene, atune with the sweet music of the angelic choir, this human side is so naturally portrayed that it leads critics to see in it the chief charm of the picture. Note the simple dress or tunics of the shepherds, the flowing draperies of the choir, the working garb of the father, and the characteristic mantle and underdress of the mother, and the staff suggestive of the shepherd's calling. See the effect of the earthly light and shadowy landscape through the doorway. Are we not impressed with the beauty and grace of the setting, the more because an artificial grandeur is lacking?

3. **Arrangement.** Observe the perfect plan of the picture, the beauty and grace of the arrangement. There are four parts to the composition; the mother and child most prominently placed, the group of shepherds, the angel host and Joseph, active in the doorway. The lighting is the most important unifying agency. How unmistakably our interest centers at once upon the form of the Christ-Child. Here is the highest light of the picture and from the little figure it radiates to every part of the canvas. Observe the line in which our interest travels, centering first upon the babe, then lifted to the mother's face, next traveling to the unaffected happiness of the shepherdess who gestures so naively, next to the rapturous expression of the young herdsman, thence to the face of the old shepherd awed by the occasion, now lifted suddenly and easily to the joyous forms of the angel band, and finally brought to earth and reality again as it rests upon the father.

How smoothly our interest travels from point to point, yet all the while keeping in the first place the supreme figure of the scene. Note the part which the attitude of the chief figures play in emphasizing the center of interest. Although the artist has not made this the chief unifying feature, it contributes much to that end. If we look at any part of the composition we are directed either by the attention of the people or the lines of objects to the center of interest. Follow the direction of the line of rocks in the lower right foreground, and the brace supporting the manger, the attention of the shepherdess, the pointing hand of the chief form of the choir, and the arm of the father. The vertical line of the column is significant of power and solemnity; the horizontal line in the position of the babe signifies quiet and repose. There is, too, a pleasing graceful effect in the suggestion of a continuous line rounding off the corners and enclosing the action of the picture. There is a very readable expression in the faces—the adoring look of the mother unaffected by the light, the pleased, naive expression of the shepherdess, the rapturous attention of one herdsman and the awed look of the other, and the listening attitude of the dog. There is a special significance in the wheat straw, and in the doves carried by the shepherdess.

Classify the details which give a divine aspect to the picture, and those which give the human side. Note the various means by which the accessories are subordinated to the central figure, and the arrangement of the outer groups serving to hold the attention within the margin. Note the impression of depth in the picture, the space that exists between the several groupings. There are no rough corners in the composition, no abrupt steps in the line of interest. The figure S is significant as a line of beauty. Point out a number of examples of such a line in this composition.

4. **Center of Interest.** The Christ-Child is the center of interest. Can you follow the methods used by the artist in emphasizing it?

5. **Light and Color.** Much of the popularity of *Holy Night* is due to the arrangement of the light. Although the radiance about the Child has been represented in other pictures, Correggio's execution is the most successful. When twilight darkens the Dresden Gallery and the other pictures become dim, this picture is said to be distinct in its own illumination. It has been observed that the lighting is the chief unifyng feature. In this scene the source of light is unusual. Observe its brilliant supernatural qualities. This subject is a fine example of gradation. Proceeding from the Child, the light penetrates with less and less brilliancy to the shadows, it also determines the order of the importance of the subordinate figures in the expression of the theme. Observe the contrast of the cold, gray light of the dawn just beginning to touch the distant hilltops, with that within the ruins. Note that there is no spot

in total darkness to modify the general brightness of the painting.

6. **Supreme Idea.** The dominant idea of the artist is beautifully expressed in the hymn *Silent Night:*

> Silent night! Holy night!
> All is calm, all is bright,
> Round yon Virgin mother and child!
> Holy infant so tender and mild,
> Sleep in heavenly peace,—
> Sleep in heavenly peace.
>
> Silent night! Holy night!
> Shepherds quake at the sight!
> Glories stream from Heaven **afar,**
> Heavenly hosts sing Alleluia
> Christ, the Saviour is born,—
> Christ, the Saviour is born.
>
> Silent night! Holy night!
> Son of God, love's pure light,
> Radiant beams from Thy holy face,
> With the dawn of redeeming grace,
> Jesus, Lord, at Thy birth,
> Jesus, Lord, at Thy birth.
>
> —Michael Hayden

7. **Color.** We who see only prints of famous paintings cannot enjoy the harmony of color which so often forms the strong feature of the picture. The effect of the penetrating light in making the color tones contribute to the general unity of the picture is marked. The mother is attired in a soft blue underdress, crimson robe and deep blue mantle. The old shepherd wears a dull red tunic. The angels are robed in a low tone of red and green.

8. **History.** The commission for *Holy Night,* sometimes called *The Adoration of the Shepherds,* was placed with Correggio, October 10, 1522. It was painted at the order of Alberto Pratoneri for the altar of his chapel in the church of San Prospero, Reggio, near the home of the artist. In 1640, the citizens of Reggio were horrified on learning that this picture had been secretly stolen by order of Duke Francesco and taken to Mod-

ena. Augustus III of Andover purchased it in 1745 with ninety-eight other subjects for $65,000. Later it became the property of the Dresden Gallery. Size: eight feet, five inches by six feet, two inches.

Holy Night is one of the twelve world pictures.

QUESTIONS

What is this picture about? How many people do you see? What are they doing? Who is the little baby? What is the expression on the mother's face? Name the different people in the picture in the order in which you see them. Are the expressions on all the faces the same? Do you think the artist had to use more thought in giving each face a different expression? Is the mother affected by the light? Is the shepherdess? Why do you suppose the shepherdess screens her eyes, although the mother does not? At what is the younger man looking? The old shepherd? How do we know these men are shepherds? Is there music in the picture? Where? Is there joy in the picture? Where? What is the father doing? What seems to be the feeling of all the people gathered here? Why are they so happy? In whom do they seem most interested? Who is the most important person in the picture? Why do you think so? Who is the next most important person? Why? How does the artist show this? What domestic animals are shown here? What impression do they add to the scene? What would be the effect if they were left out? What thoughts do you have as you study the picture? Does it appeal to the eye or to the feeling? Where did the artist get his idea for this picture? What one thing is he trying to tell us in it? What good qualities of the artist does it reveal? What are the points of beauty in the picture? What do you like most about it? Why?

THE ARTIST

Correggio, *Kor red'jō* (1494—1534), an Italian painter whose family name was Antonio Allegri. He was born in Correggio near Modena, Italy, and the name which he assumed as an artist was derived from his birthplace. But little is known of his life. He was a pupil of Blanchi, of Costa, of Lombardi and of Dossi, and his earliest works show the influence of these artists. In 1526, he began a series of paintings in the Cathedral of Parma, and many of his most noted religious subjects were executed here. In 1530, he returned to Correggio, where he worked during the remainder of his life.

Correggio was one of the five most eminent Italian painters, ranking with Michelangelo, Raphael and Titian. He excelled in religious and mythological subjects, and his works are among the most highly prized paintings of the world. The *Madonna with St. Francis* is in the Royal Gallery, Dresden; the *Marriage of St. Catherine* in the Louvre, Paris; *The Virgin Adoring the Christ-Child* in the Uffizi Gallery, Florence.

Correggio was a painter of striking individuality. . . . he was simple, almost childlike, in his thought, having little care for the religious, the classic, or the intellectual. . . . To live and be glad in the sunlight, to be simple, frank, natural and graceful, apparently made up his sum of existence in art. He would have no solemnity, no austerity, no great intellectuality. . . . Nothing tragic or mournful or pathetic interested him.
—J. C. Van Dyke

Correggio was the first to represent completely and perfectly the reality of general nature. . . . Instead of monumental construction he gives us picturesque grouping; instead of rhythm of line the harmonious play of light and shade; and with him charm and grace take the place of a grand and classic purity of style.—J. Burckhardt

THE DIVINE SHEPHERD

Murillo

Christ watches me, His little lamb;
  Cares for me day and night,
That I may be His own in heaven;
  So angels, clad in white,
Shall sing their ''Glory, glory''
  For my sake in the height.

—Christina G. Rossetti, *A Christmas Carol*

THE PICTURE

Once upon a time a certain shepherd led his flock of one
hundred sheep to the mountains. He was a good shepherd—
strong, brave and true. He loved his sheep and cared for them
tenderly. His great rugged body was bent and his face was
browned and careworn from a long life of service for them.

All day long he led them, here to the greenest pastures, there
to the purest water. All day long, too, in quiet security, the
gentle sheep fed upon the fresh grass. When the shades of
evening began to fall, the old shepherd, thankful for the close
of day, gathered his flock for the homeward walk.

But when he had counted the sheep, he stopped, perplexed.
Could he have made a mistake? Once more he numbered them,
slowly, carefully. Again he reached ninety and nine, but he
counted no further. The hundredth sheep was not there.

Dark clouds appeared in the west. Night was almost upon
him. He waited but a moment. He looked to where the ninety
and nine were huddled together. Then he turned, and far
back up the mountain he hurried. Behind him the sheep
bleated piteously.

Over cliff and through thicket he pushed his way. Suddenly
a glad shout rang out. The lost sheep was found! Tenderly

196

THE DIVINE SHEPHERD.—*Murillo*

the good shepherd lifted it to his shoulders and hurried to where the ninety and nine were waiting.

It has been a long, long time since that day in old Judea when Jesus told this story of the Good Shepherd. But in all these years that beautiful thought has lived in the hearts of men.

Like sweet music, it has touched the soul of poet and painter, living in the songs of one, and in the pictures of the other. Can anything be more charming than the thought of a certain painter who made the Christ-Child the good shepherd of this picture? Once the Saviour said, "And a little child shall lead them," and true to this thought the artist has pictured for us the shepherd in the person of the boy Jesus.

What a charm this simple scene has for us! A little face looks out from the soft light of the painting with an expression so childlike and winning that at once we feel ourselves drawn to it. Jesus, fresh from his play in the fields, his round, healthy, little body full of a life which even the coarse sheepskin garment cannot hide, is resting near his sheep. One chubby hand holds a shepherd's crook, the other rests upon the head of a favorite lamb. The flock of sheep are feeding quietly in the background.

Observe the poise of the head, the clustering curls, the dimpled chin and the simple, childish dignity. Full of expression, the dark eyes reflect his serious thoughts. "True eyes" are they

> Too pure and too honest in aught to disguise
> The sweet soul shining through them.

How natural he is! There is as yet no look of divine wisdom, no expression of compassion to lift him out of the vale of care-free childhood. Just to be a simple, happy, fun-loving, barefoot boy he is quite content. Whittier and Longfellow have each described such a lad.

While we may be sure that no idea of kingly birth or of his own great mission has a place in this child's thoughts, yet is there not a suggestion of his divinity? "A homely scene with a heavenly meaning."

All too swiftly will pass these boyhood days. Are we not made to feel by the presence of the sheep the child's mission when he becomes a man? As the Saviour of the world he will say to the multitudes about him:

I am the good shepherd; the good shepherd giveth his life for his sheep. I am the good shepherd, and know my sheep, and am known of mine. As the Father knoweth me, even so know I the Father, and I lay down my life for my sheep.

How beautiful is the light which beams full upon and softens the scene. Flooding with a bright, warm glow the face and form of the child, it slips away in the shadows.

But study as we will the different points of interest, our thought always returns to the one central figure. The warm glow of sky above, the full, rich tones of foliage and crumbling wall behind are themselves but the lesser ornaments of a setting in which a lovely vision of childhood rests.

> Is it warm in that green valley,
>   Vale of childhood, where you dwell?
> Is it calm in that green valley,
>   Round whose bowers such great hills swell?
> Are there giants in the valley—
>   Giants leaving foot-prints yet?
> Are there angels in the valley?
>   Tell me—I forget.
>   —Jean Ingelow

PLAN FOR STUDY

1. **Source of Subject.** "Murillo," writes Curtis, "is supposed to have been indebted for this design to an engraving of Cupid by Della-Bella, which is found in an edition of the Metamorphoses of Ovid."

The subject represents more than all else the Saviour's words, "And a little child shall lead them."

2. **Setting.** A landscape with sheep in the background and foliage to the left. What does the ruin suggest? The sheep? Note the sheepskin garment and the crook, suggestive of the shepherd's calling. What effect is added by the presence of the lamb?

3. **Arrangement.** The figures are arranged in a triangle. Note the arrangement of the simple details of the setting, which, while adding much to the impression, are nevertheless subordinated to the child's figure. The center of interest is here made the dominant figure by its position and size, the subordination of lesser objects, such as the sheep indistinct in the background, the foliage, and the pet lamb, the lighting, which is brightest on the boy, and the motive itself.

4. **Center of Interest.** Note the means by which the artist makes the boy the dominant figure. Were the sheep painted more distinctly, our interest might be divided between the child and the sheep.

5. **Light.** The light comes from the front at the left, and, lighting the child, passes to the subordinate figures in the background. The foliage at the left is in deep shadow, the ruin is indistinct. The lighting is after the second style of the artist —that of warm coloring. The child is clad in a red tunic and a garment of sheepskin.

6. **Location.** This picture hangs in the Prado Museum, Madrid, Spain. Size three feet by four feet.

COMMENT

His renderings of child life are always most happy; the Christ-Child possesses a charming mixture of divine and human expression.—Hoyt

Look at his Virgins, whose beauty is of so human a cast; his infant Christs, whose grace is so much more carnal than divine; his angels and cherubs, which might have been the despair of Boucher and his school; his saints and monks, who adore the Madonna or the Christ-Child with such earthly passion.—Carl Justi

QUESTIONS

What is this picture about? What is the little child doing? How does he show his love for the lamb? Where is he seated? What is the expression on his face? Of what does he seem to be thinking? What does he carry in his hand? Why? What is the lamb doing? Of what does it seem to be thinking? Why do you suppose the lamb has come to the child? Are there other sheep in the picture? What are they doing? Can you see them very plainly? Why not? Are you much interested in them? In whom are you more interested? Why? What are the beautiful qualities of the child? What kind of thoughts does he seem to have? What are your thoughts as you view the picture? Where is the brightest light? Can you tell from what direction it comes? How? What are the most pleasing things about the picture? What do you think the artist is trying to say to us in this picture? Does it tell you anything about his character? What?

THE ARTIST

Murillo, *Mū-ril'ō,* **Bartolomé Estéban** (1618—1682), a celebrated Spanish painter, was born at Seville, Spain.

From his uncle, to whom he was early apprenticed, he learned the essentials of his art. Little is known of his early life. He was an orphan at eleven, and life to him was a weary struggle until he reached manhood.

Learning easily, he soon outstripped his master, who, when the artist was twenty-two years old, left him to struggle alone. Forced to earn his own living, he painted worthless pictures and sold them in the market place. He went to Madrid in 1643 and became a pupil of Velasquez, who was then at the height of his career. He returned to Seville in 1645, where he painted a series of pictures that brought him general recognition. He established the public Academy at Seville in 1660. He was made court painter by Charles II, although he still insisted upon remaining in Seville. There is a list of about 418 of his paintings.

Simple in manner and taste, deeply religious and generous to a fault, he was the most popular artist of his time in Spain. His pictures fall under three styles: 1. In his early career he painted in the "cold style" in those pictures mostly genre. 2. After coming under the influence of Velasquez, his pictures are warmer in color, "warm style." 3. For his religious conceptions he developed a soft glow or "misty style."

Other pictures: *St. Anthony of Padua,* Seville Museum; *Jesus and John the Baptist,* Madrid; *Immaculate Conception,* Louvre, Paris; and *The Melon Eaters,* Munich.

CHRIST IN THE TEMPLE

Hofmann

THE PICTURE

Again the year had rolled around, and Passover week, the time when all Jewish families that could do so made their annual journey to Jerusalem, was at hand.

Miles away in the little town of Nazareth, usually so quiet and serene in its sheltered place among the hills, Joseph and Mary and the boy Jesus were in the bustle and excitement of preparing for the annual journey. It was an occasion of great rejoicing to this family. Twelve years had passed since the glorious tidings of the Christ-Child's birth were heralded by angels on Bethlehem's plain. During most of this time the holy family had lived in their little cottage in Nazareth. Here Joseph worked industriously in his shop, and amid the lowly surroundings of the carpenter's home the Christ-Child

Had all that infant care beguiles,
And early knew his mother in her smiles.

Like other Jewish lads, Jesus was taught from the Law and the Prophets, the book from which he first learned to read. He had also memorized many passages from these same writings. Often had his mother told him of the great city of Jerusalem. Often had he listened in wonder as she described the Temple there, and longed for the time to come when he, too, might worship in its courts. Now as a youth of twelve the fond hopes of a happy childhood were to be realized. The time at which he should be presented in the Temple had arrived. How the heart of the boy bounded with delight at the very thought!

The glory and brightness of a summer's day dawned upon

CHRIST IN THE TEMPLE.—*Hofmann*

all the region about Jerusalem. Nature seemed inclined to help on this joyous occasion. Amid vast throngs of pilgrims the family journeyed to the holy city. With hymns of rejoicing the great company entered the city's gates. Yonder, on Mount Moriah, stood the Temple with its Royal Porch and columns of Corinthian marble. Jesus knew it as the object of his boyhood dreams, the house of God.

To this place Jesus came near the close of the third day. There, grand and majestic in their robes of office, the doctors and rabbis were wont to explain the Scriptures to worshippers gathered in the courts. For hours the child stood, awed by the wisdom of these wonderful men. But hark! The reply of an aged rabbi to a countryman nearby startled him. It was wrong!

Quickly he pushed through the throng and took his stand in their midst. How astounded they were at the strange sight of this country lad disputing the answer of a gray-haired rabbi. There was a divine intelligence in his eyes which awed them. More amazing still, his words, spoken in the sweetest and clearest of voices, showed wonderful wisdom. His answers cast light upon Scriptures, the like of which had never been heard in that holy place.

All eyes were turned upon him in astonishment. In that company were aged doctors versed in all the lore of the heavens; great philosophers and grand old rabbis grown white in the search for truth. Question after question was asked him. He answered them all with a fluency and earnestness that could not be doubted. Like messages direct from God, the words of the boy pierced the clouds of their understanding.

Meanwhile the festivities had ended. Joseph and Mary with relatives and neighbors began the homeward journey. In the throngs which surged through the gates the family became separated, and they went a day's journey before they learned that Jesus was not in the company. In great fear they hastened back to the city and began their search for the missing boy. Great was their joy when, after long and fruitless endeavor, they discovered in one of the remotest rooms of the Temple their boy among the doctors. Very simply he replied to their gentle reproaches, "How is it that ye sought me? Wist ye not that I must be about my Father's business?"

Gathered in one of the courts of the magnificent building, and regardless of all surroundings, the astonished doctors are gazing with various expressions of wonder at the Divine Child in their midst. He is the central figure of the group. He stands with outstretched hand pointing to the aged questioner, whom he is answering in the sweetest voice imaginable.

What varied expressions the faces of the doctors present. The old rabbi to the right is sitting in rapt attention with the air of one who is diligently seeking after truth. Imagine his surprise when in answer to a difficult question put by him, Jesus promptly gives a reply. Perhaps he doubts the statement Jesus has made. Mechanically turning the pages of the volume resting upon his knees, he is searching for some argument with which to puzzle the Child. How interested the other members of the group seem to be. Perhaps each of them in turn questioned the boy, only to be answered with divine wisdom.

Somewhat apart from the group is a listener in whose face there is every evidence of a stern and stubborn character. The radiant purity of the boy's face, the sweet childish voice, find no answering chord within him. Stern, unrelenting, combative, he stands squarely upon his faith, regarding Jesus with none too friendly a look. The book of his religion forms a support for his arm in much the same manner that it holds his creed. To him it is the rock upon which no child, however divinely inspired, can make the least impression. With the other hand he grasps a scroll of the Law. In the person of this stern Pharisee we have the type of a people upon whom the gentle pleadings of a kingly Saviour had no effect.

What a pleasant contrast is the mild, gentle face of the white-bearded old rabbi. With both hands pressed upon a stout cane, he regards the Christ with the pleased wonder of a very old man who is looking upon a young and witty child.

In the keen philosopher next to the old rabbi, we have a younger man, broad-minded and intellectual. The occasion fills him with delight. There is a kindliness in his manner and a respectful attitude in his bearing which gains our friendship at once. Anxious to interrupt the speaker for only a moment, he hesitates, restrained as though in the presence of a king.

But in the divine loveliness of the Christ there rests the supreme attraction of the picture. Clad in a white tunic, symbolic of purity, innocence and gentleness, he stands in the midst of these men as the nearest approach to our ideal of the Saviour as a youth. Regardless of the stern disfavor of the Pharisee, he rests his arm upon the desk which supports the Scriptures. With hand outstretched, his dark, lustrous eyes look directly into those of the questioner. There is a contentment in his bearing, a satisfaction in knowing that his duty is being well performed. He is in his Father's house. He is there in the interest of his Father's business. The supreme moment in his boyhood has been reached.

PLAN FOR STUDY

1. **Source of Subject.** The finding of the boy Jesus in the Temple with the doctors as told in the account of St. Luke. This incident in the boyhood of the Saviour was always a favorite one with the old masters.

2. **Setting.** This is first of all a figure picture. The artist has given but little attention to the background, which is only vaguely indicated. There is, however, a suggestion of magnificence in the half-hidden marble pillars and pedestals. Note the effect of the scroll and the open book in contributing to the impression of learning, thought and discussion. The pure white tunic of Jesus is in striking contrast to the costly robes of the doctors. Is not this a happy touch, tending to heighten the effect of the Child's individuality? The richly covered desk and the carved chair add a touch of magnificence to the scene. The costumes of the doctors are partly Roman and partly Oriental.

3. **Arrangement.** Various methods of arranging the Christ-Child and the doctors have been followed by different painters, but it is generally conceded that the arrangement in this canvas by Hofmann is by far the most effective and pleasing.

The vertical lines, typifying dignity and solemnity, are pre-dominant. There is a sufficient variety of lines, however, to make the general effect pleasing. Our interest centers at once on the face and gesture of the Child, then follows the direction of his arm, travels along the open book and across the faces of the three men on the right, pauses for a moment on the features of the one on the extreme left, studies the stern disfavor of the man in the left foreground and returns again to the chief figure. The chief charm of the picture rests in the character expressed in the faces.

4. **Center of Interest.** We do not need to be told that the center of interest in this composition is the Christ-Child. This is indicated by the attention of all the people in the scene focused upon him. Note how the lighting is also one of the unifying features. Then, too, the title and motive of the composition require that the Child have a central position in the group.

5. **Light and Shade.** The lighting is one of the chief unifying features. It falls upon the form of the Christ-Child with such fine effect that engravers often exclude all other figures and accessories and represent only the figure of the youthful Christ. The artist was not always so successful in his light and shade effects, but this picture shows him at his best.

6. **Supreme Motive.** The artist's supreme motive was to idealize Jesus as a youth.

7. **History.** This picture was painted in 1882 and exhibited the following year. It now hangs in the Dresden Gallery.

QUESTIONS

What is this picture about? What do the men seem to be doing? Who are they? Why have they come to this place? In whom do they seem most interested? What seems to be their feelings? What is the Christ-Child doing? To which of the doctors does he seem to be speaking? How does this doctor act? Is he convinced? Why do you say this? Are the expressions on all the faces alike? Is it more pleasing to have them all different? Was it harder for the artist to make them so? In which one of the doctors are you most interested? Why? Do you see any background in the picture? Why did not the artist make it more distinct? What is the chief figure in the picture? Why does his form stand out so strongly? Are you pleased with this picture? Does the Christ-Child seem perfectly at home among these stern men? What do you suppose makes him so courageous? What are some of the beautiful qualities of this picture? What is the most pleasing thing about it? What thoughts do you have as you study it?

THE ARTIST

Hof'mann, Heinrich Johann (1824—1902), a German historical painter, was born at Darmstadt. He was a pupil of Hildebrandt and Schadow at the Academy of Dusseldorf and Antwerp. In 1862 he became a professor in the Academy at Dresden, where he still lives and works. His pictures are in the Dresden Theatre and Gallery; the National Gallery, Berlin; and in private collections. His other pictures of note are *Christ Taken Prisoner*, Dresden; *Christ and the Rich Young Ruler,* and *Christ Preaching from a Skiff,* Berlin.

His *Christ in the Temple* is deservedly famous.—Addison

It is not only one of the best of Hofmann's pictures, but it seems to us one of the most pleasing among the many representations of the subject. —Cook

In color, composition and drawing his paintings are good, though not of first rank; they owe their popularity to his ideal conception of biblical events.

THE LAST SUPPER

Leonardo da Vinci

Now when the even was come, he sat down with the twelve.

And as they were eating, Jesus took bread, and blessed it, and brake it, and gave it to the disciples, and said, Take, eat; this is my body.

And he took the cup, and gave thanks, and gave it to them, saying, Drink ye all of it;

For this is my blood of the new testament, which is shed for many for the remission of sins.

But I say unto you, I will not drink henceforth of this fruit of the vine, until that day when I drink it new with you in my Father's kingdom.

—Matthew xxvi:20, 26—29

THE PICTURE

It is the night of the Passover supper. Here in this small upper room of a house in Jerusalem Jesus and His disciples are partaking of the evening meal.

Today, while all Palestine is stirred with the celebration of the deliverance of the people of Israel from the cruel bondage in Egypt, the Saviour has journeyed with great throngs to the Holy City. Now seated with those whom he loves so well, He is breaking the bread of the farewell feast.

Through the open window the Judean hills lie silvered in the moonlight. Gentle winds bring to the little company the sweet perfume of the springtime. But the happiness of this bright season finds no answering chord in the souls of these men. They are sorrowful, amazed, horrified. What can it mean?

St. Matthew tells us. Jesus has just spoken. Not that these are His first words, for he has talked to them all evening. And oh, how sadly he speaks. As the disciples listen a feeling

209

of awe which they themselves cannot explain steals over them. In the dim glow of the lamps the words of Jesus as he sits in their midst seem full of a strange meaning—a suggestion that he is about to leave them.

But what is He just now saying? Eagerly they bend toward Him. Do they hear aright? Surely there is some mistake. "Verily I say unto you," Jesus is speaking mournfully, "that one of you shall betray me." The beauty of the night and the calm peacefulness of the scene are lost as the disciples start up in amazement.

"One of you shall betray me!" All the pent-up love of the disciples finds expression in the cry, "Lord, is it I?" How anxiously they seek to know, each in his own way, the meaning of the awful words! With what feelings of love, sorrow and astonishment they implore the Saviour to explain.

In the group to the left, Peter, quite in keeping with his hasty temper, bends far forward and begs of John to ask of the Saviour who the traitor can be. There is all of the recklessness and impulsiveness of Peter in his movement and gesture. Not content with merely asking, he grasps the shoulder of John in his excitement, while his other hand, in which he holds a knife, quite unconsciously jerks forward and strikes Judas in the back.

Can there be any question as to the real traitor? Was ever a more admirable representation of him made? This black-haired, swarthy-skinned man over whose face a shadow falls as black as his own great sin itself can be no other than Judas.

With one hand outstretched on the table, the other tightly clutching the money bag, he looks up in great alarm. The touch of the knife in Peter's hand has filled him with fright. He clutches the sack of silver more tightly, his elbow in the movement upsetting the salt, which we know to be the old Roman sign of an approaching quarrel.

In what contrast to the cunning, hateful, determined profile of the traitor are the pure, delicate features of John. His is a broken-hearted silence. There is no trace of hatred or desire for revenge in his manner. True to his own pure, loving disposition he is wonderfully gentle in his grief.

THE LAST SUPPER.—*Leonardo Da Vinci*

But if revenge is threatened in the action of Peter, what strong feelings of another character are expressed in the gestures of the group to the right. Here suspicion, horror and hate are all suggested in their violent movements. They can hardly believe the terrible words. Again they implore the Saviour to explain.

Here Thomas is beckoning to Him by raising his finger to his forehead as he asks the oft-repeated "Lord, is it I?" In front of him James the elder with arms outstretched expresses his horror at such a detestable thing. But if John, in the right group, is lovely in his calm sorrow, how fine is the character of Philip, who bends over his companions with deep regret written on his gentle features.

To the right of this group, at the end of the long table, three other men are talking together. The figure so full of the dignity which comes with age and experience is Simon, who listens astonished and dismayed. Yet how well, in contrast with the others, he conceals his feelings.

Matthew at his right is replying to him and is the most aroused disciple of the group. Thaddeus stands next to him, and is full of energy as he points toward the Saviour in his earnest conversation.

Here at the opposite end, Bartholomew is bending eagerly forward to catch the words of the others. Next to him James the younger reaches out his left hand to touch the shoulder of Peter, who in turn seeks to arouse John.

Plainly this group is working to arouse John to question the Saviour. They seem to think that if John, whom they know to be the Master's favorite, will but ask Him, He will answer. Behind Peter, Andrew, full of horror, seems powerless to move. He can only express his feelings by his upraised hands.

Thus from the sunniness of youth to the shadows of age, from the deepest sorrow to the eager spirit of revenge, this company of men are arrayed before us true to life. Their hands speak the words they cannot utter; in their faces is mirrored that love for the Master which they just now are so anxious to show.

But supreme over all is the Christ, the central figure. On

either side the disciples have drawn away for the moment in their surprise, leaving Him quite alone in their midst.

Did ever artist's brush paint a face so sad, so submissive, so forgiving, so divine? With what surprise we learn that the painter left this wonderful face to his mind incomplete. Long did he think about this face, longer about it than any other part of the picture, but his hand always trembled, and his confidence always wavered, when he endeavored to complete it. ''I cannot hope to see the face of Christ, except in Paradise,'' Leonardo wrote to Lodovico Pforza.

> Vainly my pencil struggles to express
> The sorrowing grandeur of such holiness
> In patient thought, in ever seeking prayer
> I strive to shape that glorious face within;
> But the soul's mirror dulled and dimmed by sin
> Reflects not yet the perfect image there.
>
> —William Story

PLAN FOR STUDY

1. **Source of Subject.** The Last Supper is one of the earliest and most often painted themes in Christian art. As early as the 11th century the subject was pictured in Italian churches. The Jewish passover commemorates the deliverance of the Israelites out of the bondage in Egypt. Jesus in the last day of His ministry on earth desired that this observance should mark His farewell supper with His disciples. Accordingly Peter and John arranged for it. They secured an upper chamber, authorized the preparation of the sacrifice in the temple and purchased wine, herbs, fruit, vinegar and unleavened bread. Before night all had been arranged. The twelve had bathed in ceremonial preparation and were assembled at the appointed hour.

A feeling of unusual suspense pervaded the company. Plainly the Saviour was ''troubled in spirit.'' An inward struggle was going on in His soul; no mortal mind could conceive how great that struggle was. Then the tragic moment came, and the Saviour announced His betrayal. That moment lives in this conception of Leonardo da Vinci.

2. **Setting.** Time: Thursday night, April, A. D. 34. Place: An upper chamber in a house in Jerusalem. Windows in the rear wall frame bits of landscape. A rare touch is this which gives the pent-up feelings an outlet into the calm, beautiful night. On the table are the prescribed portions of food and wine. The location of the painting on the wall of the refectory or dining room of the Monastery of Santa Maria delle Grazie, in Milan, adds much to its effectiveness. Naturally the choice of the subject for a convent dining hall was a happy one. The painting occupies the entire breadth of the narrow room. Ten feet below the three tables of the prior and the monks are arranged along the room parallel to the one in the painting. The cloth and dishes in the painting are identical with those of the convent tables.

3. **Arrangement.** The composition of this painting is its chief claim to a lasting place in art. Indeed, little else now remains of the *Last Supper*. A difficult task confronted the artist in representing this subject. Although the Last Supper had been painted often, no really great composition up to this time had been produced. Early artists like da Vinci had chosen the dramatic moment immediately following the Saviour's announcement of His betrayal, but none, like da Vinci, had portrayed the assembled company in a manner wholly removed from the conventional.

By conventional here is meant an arrangement after a set rule and an unnatural one. Nature abhors monotony; the human eye seeks always to avoid it. Truly great artists recognize this principle and are governed accordingly. Da Vinci's problem was the grouping of thirteen figures around a long table in such a way as to avoid a monotonous flow of line. A long row is unavoidably monotonous.

We know that da Vinci planned for variety here. Proof of this is one of his recently discovered notebooks, which was found to contain a page of entries providing for just this thing in great detail. Under the various names of the disciples he jotted down characteristic gestures and expressions which should be called forth by the Saviour's announcement. A variety of emotions was planned in order that no two men would act alike. He provided next in these plans for a variety of positions. To accomplish this He divided the company into four groups of three each. These are arranged along the table placed sidewise and not endwise.

The direction of the table is in itself an effective contribution to the composition. Why? Note the variety of expressions set forth by the different groups. At the right end, the three, Matthew, Thaddeus and Simon, all talk earnestly together, apparently deaf to sounds outside their own immediate circle. Here discussion is the dominant theme. James the elder, Thomas and Philip, next to them, gaze stupefied. Here each man is self-occupied, quite in contrast to the fraternal feeling in the discussion at the right. Each asks his particular question in his own particular way. Yet as a group they express a composite feeling of horror mingled with astonishment.

John, Judas and Peter draw together in what is generally thought to be the most striking and most nearly perfect of the groups. Theirs is an apparent momentary union of spirits. Peter is intensely interested in what John will do; Judas certainly is not less so. There is action here, too, in the aggressive attitude of Peter, and the terrified drawing back of the traitor. James the younger, Bartholomew and Andrew, at the left end, are a passive group. The interest is a breathless one, however, as they await the effect of Peter's suggestion to John.

A keen insight into the hearts of men is here revealed. Twelve men are represented. Each has heard the tragic words. Each shows the effect upon him in a way most indicative of his true character. The problem of adequately expressing such emotion was a difficult one. Much is expressed here in the gesture of the hands—a characteristic essentially Italian. Peter as a disciple was forward at times, vain, impetuous, straight-forward, sincere, quick-tempered, warm-hearted, brave, aggressive. Do you find any evidence of these qualities here? John and James, known as "Sons of Thunder," were youthful, tender-hearted, imaginative, pure and powerful. John was gentle and loving, the favorite disciple of his Master; James was zealous, passionate and fiery. Has the artist here caught essentially these qualities? Bartholomew was scholarly; Matthew, practical; Thomas, brave and inclined to distrust. Do you find these qualities represented here?

The revealing of individual character and group expression, however, was not the real problem of the composition. We have seen that the artist has in this composition secured variety. Yet the artist might go too far in this, so far that his composition might fall to pieces. A truly great picture seeks to give but one impression. That is the true test always. Note how the artist here has met that test. Though there are in this company masterful characters, he has yet represented in their midst One, a Master of them all. Da Vinci has here created a personality which draws to it every individual in the company. This is accomplished in two ways. First there is a mental unity, and second, there is a unity of physical lines. A single thought is the exciting force in this company. However varied the expressions and attitudes of these men, a single impulse moves them individually and collectively to ask "Lord, is it I?" Then observe how the physical lines direct us to the center of interest. Matthew, the dominant personality of the group at the head of the table, extends his right arm and directs us to the subject of his thought. Both he and Thaddeus look at Simon and Simon in turn directs our gaze also to the same subject of thought. We look at the individuals in the group next to them, and they are gazing directly at the central figure. Peter, at the opposite end, leaning far over to speak to John, connects with his body the group at the end with the group on the immediate left of the center. Though John, in the coveted place at the right hand of his Master, bends away with downcast look, Peter's hand serves to counteract the tendency his averted gaze would have in directing our interest from the central figure. Look where we will in the composition, we are directed by physical or mental lines to the supreme figure.

4. **Center of Interest.** We need not be told that the Christ is the center of interest. The emotions of the artist as he here set down his conception of the Saviour's personality may well be imagined. For days at a time he would remain before the

work long after the other figures and accessories had been completed and wrestle with his emotions before the unfinished face of the Saviour. At times he would rush out of the convent, not to return until after several days of wandering through the streets. Once he sought the advice of Bernardo Zenale: "O Leonardo," his friend replied, "the error into which thou hast fallen is one from which only the Divine Being Himself can deliver thee; for it is not in thy power, nor in that of anyone else, to give greater divinity and beauty to any figures than thou hast done to these. . . . Therefore be of good cheer, and leave the Christ imperfect; for thou wilt never be able to accomplish the Saviour after such Apostles."

Da Vinci followed his advice, and the downcast eyes giving an indefinable expression to the Saviour's face are a positive triumph in the suggestiveness which they contribute to His features. By suggestion here is meant the power of the face to awaken our imagination and to stir our emotions. Quite alone, as in all the tragic moments of his ministry, the Christ seems to be searching His inward Self. What pathos in His isolation! In this agonizing moment His beloved followers are powerless to comfort Him. They who ply Him with only vain questionings can never realize in their mortal weakness the intensity of His suffering.

5. **Color.** As will be noted in the historical data included, the artist was most unfortunate in his method of painting this picture. He ignored the established method of fresco painting, and mixed his colors with oil to secure a brighter effect. One can get no definite idea of the original coloring from the present painting, retouched as it has been by a number of mediocre painters.

6. **History.** From an entry in the convent records by the architect for "works in the refectory where Leonardo is painting the Apostles," under date of 1497, we have the first record of the painting. It was ordered by Lodovico Maria Sforza, Duke of Milan, for the wall of the refectory in the Monastery of Santa delle Grazie as a memorial to his saintly wife Beatrice, who often worshipped here. In 1498 Fra Luca Paciolo notes in his journal its completion. Francis I of France, in control

of Milan in 1515, was struck with the beauty of the painting. He tried to arrange the impossible feat of its removal to France and had to content himself with a copy by Luini. The painting, owing to its rapid deterioration, was retouched in 1726 by Bellotti; 1770, Mazza; 1804, Amoretti; 1853, Barozzi. The latest effort at restoration was made in 1908.

Lomazzo mourned the painting as "utterly ruined" in 1585. In 1624, C. Sanese regretted its almost total destruction, and Taine, in 1866, said, "The *Last Supper* is no longer visible."

The monks in the 18th century had a door made through the lower part, removing the feet of the Saviour. Napoleon's cavalry, in 1796, stabled their horses in the hall and amused themselves by throwing missiles at the painting. The monastery was flooded in 1800, with disastrous results to the picture. During the Austrian rule in Lombardy the national arms were nailed on the wall above the head of Christ. The general plan, unsurpassed in any painting, is all that remains of the original. Some excellent photographs have been made, that of Raphael Morghen's in 1800, from a copy by Marco d'Oggione, being justly popular. The picture is 28 feet long. The figures are one-half more than lifesize.

> Tho' searching damps and many an envious flaw
> Have marred this work; the calm ethereal grace,
> The love deep-seated in the Saviour's face,
> The mercy, goodness, have not failed to awe
> The Elements; as they do melt and thaw
> The heart of the Beholder—and erase
> (At least for one rapt moment) every trace
> Of disobedience to the primal law.
> The annunciation of the dreadful truth
> Made to the Twelve, survives: lip, forehead, cheek,
> And hand reposing on the board in ruth
> Of what it utters, while the unguilty seek
> Unquestionable meanings—still bespeak
> A labor worthy of eternal youth!
>
> —William Wordsworth, *The Last Supper by da Vinci*

COMMENT

The *Last Supper* is ranked as one of the World's Pictures, a selection of twelve paintings carrying with it a rather popular sanction, but not wholly recognized as such by art critics in general.

So easily first among the achievements of Christian art.—H. H. Powers

Leonardo's picture remains the most perfect composition in the history of painting of all ages.—Richter

It has been well called the compendium of all his studies and of all his writings, and, chronologically, it is the first masterpiece of the Renaissance.

—Symonds

QUESTIONS

Where is the scene of the picture? What event has the painter here chosen for the subject of this picture? What is the exciting force in the scene? What was the artist's problem in representing this group? Does he avoid the conventional? How does he secure variety? What is secured by variety? Do you think the arrangement the most pleasing one that could be planned? Why? What is the general plan? Explain how each group is a unit? Show that these groups or units are connected and subordinated to a center of interest. Is there a variety in these group themes? Which are alike; which are unlike? Where is the center of interest? Explain in detail how each individual is drawn to this supreme personality. Make a character study of the men. What dominant qualities stand out in each? Contrast Judas and Philip; John and Peter. Which is the strongest personality of the disciples? The weakest? Does the Saviour's place at the table add to His effectiveness as a center of interest? How? How does the expression of the Saviour differ from that of the disciples in respect to singleness and clearness? What is the secret of its power to inspire the beholder? What motive, do you think, inspired this conception of the Last Supper? Is your impression of the scene a definite one? If so, how do you account for it?

THE ARTIST

Vinci, *Vin'chē,* **Leonardo da** (1452—1519), one of the world's most celebrated artists, was born at Vinci in Tuscany. His father was a lawyer. From childhood Vinci had every advantage of intellectual and artistic environment, and he exhibited at an early age those powers which led him to brilliant achievement in later years.

Vinci could sing, he could tame the wildest horses and bend the strongest iron; he painted some of the greatest pictures, and designed some of the most wonderful bridges and warships of his day. He was a botanist, a scientist and a mechanician. He was a poet as well as a painter and a sculptor as well as an architect. In fact, there was very little he could not do and do well. Seldom does **Christ** bestow so lavishly such gifts upon a single individual. He began his study with Andrea Verrocchio about 1470. Here he remained for two years studying drawing, modeling, designing for architecture, and even delving into the physical sciences. He went to Milan in 1487, lived several years in Florence, and painted for a time in Rome. In his later years he painted many portraits, *Mona Lisa,* the most famous portrait in the world, being produced in this period. Here is a bit of philosophy from his notebook:

> Who cannot do as he desires, must do
> What lies within his power.
> Vain it is
> To wish what cannot be; the wise man holds
> That from such wishing he must free himself.

Among the greatest masters of the Florentine Renaissance stands Leonardo da Vinci, side by side with Michelangelo and Raphael.—Richter

FRIEZE OF THE PROPHETS

Sargent

Life of Ages, richly poured,
Love of God, unspent and free,
Flowing in the Prophet's word
And the People's liberty.

—Samuel Johnson

THE FRIEZE

Through all the progress of the Chosen People, from the call of Abraham to the advent of the Saviour, God spoke to them through prophets. The prophets were men of great strength of character and profound religious experience. Receiving their commission directly from Jehovah, they spoke fearlessly and with authority, repeatedly warning the wayward nation of impending doom unless they forsook the worship of idols and returned to the true worship of God.

The prophets form a group of men unique in the history of the world, and as such they appealed to Sargent when he received a commission to decorate one of the rooms in the Boston Public Library.

Let us ascend the marble staircase of this magnificent library building to Sargent's Hall. Here in one grand scheme of decoration which reaches from wainscot to lunette and from lunette to grace the ceiling itself is revealed in a painting the old, old theme of Israel's confusion, oppression, deliverance and subsequent downfall.

But it is the company of heroic men—the *Frieze of the Prophets*, which most interests us. They turn to us with faces so full of expression that we would know their message.

Like a symphony which master musicians draw from their instruments—first the tender chords as of hope, dying then

221

away into the plaintive notes of despair, and again swelling to the supreme expression—breathe from these walls the spirits of those prophets of old.

What life and vigor, what real feeling, seems embodied in their forms. Stately in their full, flowing mantles, and with gestures fraught with meaning, they stand out so clear, so forceful and so lifelike that the impression they create will ever live in the mind.

Here in the central panel just over the door are the chief figures—Moses, Joshua and Elijah. Moses, majestic and awe-inspiring in his conventional robes, stands in the center holding the tables of the law. With hands resting upon the two stones, so expressive of religious and civil authority, and enveloped in the mists of the Spirit, he is indeed a fitting representative of the leader of prophets—the "Spokesman of Jehovah." "Fear not," we seem to hear him say, "for God has come to you to speak with you, that you may fear Him and do His will."

Strong and full of vigorous action, on the right is Joshua, sheathing his sword. Victorious general of many battles, he is indeed a fitting character to stand on the right hand of his leader. In his imposing figure there is no trace of weariness or inclination to shirk the tremendous task which has devolved upon him. Elijah stands on the left. With an expression and gesture of supplication he seems again at the altar in that contest with the priests of Baal, and to call, "O Lord of Israel, let it be known this day that thou art God in Israel and that I am thy servant."

In a continuous and smoothly flowing line to the right and to the left of the central panel are the other prophets of the frieze. Here to the left are Daniel, Ezekiel, Nahum and Amos.

What a variety of expression their strong faces show. Daniel with open scroll stands first. He seems composed, not despairing, only sad. In full, flowing garment and with hands clasped across his breast, Ezekiel is next in line. It is not a despairing prophet that we see in this figure, but one whose evident mission is to inspire hope.

With upraised hand Nahum stands next and is raising his

FRIEZE OF THE PROPHETS.—*Sargent*

Center Panel

voice in earnest entreaty for Israel's repentance. In flowing mantle and with hands clasped on his herdsman's crook, Amos the shepherd prophet poses as the sternest and most forboding character of the group.

Here to the right of the central panel are Jeremiah, Jonah, Isaiah and Habakkuk. All hope has left the stern old face of Jeremiah, "the weeping prophet." Apart from the others he stands in deep despair, with grief all the more hard to bear because he is so lonely.

Just behind, Jonah is reading from a scroll with the single word "Jehovah" upon it. In the figure of Isaiah many find the most impressive character of the panel. There is a questioning air in his gesture as though he were asking, "O Lord, how long?"

Rugged and stern is the figure of Habakkuk, who stands next, at the extreme right.

Zephaniah, Joel, Obadiah and Hosea are pictured in the extreme left panel. These are the prophets of despair, predicting the disaster and woe that shall surely come to Israel. Save only for the one hopeful figure of Hosea in white, the grief of these men is awful to behold.

On the extreme right and in pleasing contrast are the prophets of hope with one despairing figure, Micah. It is a glorious prophecy indeed which these strong men are giving to their people. Not only are they predicting the successful completion of the temple, but even at that early day they are foretelling the first Christmas tidings.

PLAN FOR STUDY

1. **Source of Subject.** The Frieze of the Prophets is one of three divisions of a complete decorative scheme which Sargent himself describes as representing "the triumph of religion—a mural decoration illustrating certain stages of Jewish and Christian history." The entire work consists of a frieze, a lunette and a part of the ceiling. Sargent inscribed the text of his theme above the lunette:

FRIEZE OF THE PROPHETS.—*Sargent*

Left Center

(21) They forgat God their saviour, which had done great things in Egypt; (36) And they served idols: which were a snare unto them. (37) Yea, they sacrificed their sons and their daughters unto devils, (38) And shed innocent blood, even the blood of their sons and of their daughters, . . . unto the idols of Canaan: . . . (40) Therefore was the wrath of the Lord kindled against his people, . . . (41) And he gave them into the hand of the heathen; and they that hated them ruled over them. (42) Their enemies also oppressed them, and they were brought into subjection under their hand. (44) Nevertheless he regarded their affliction, when he heard their cry: (45) And he remembered for them his covenant. —Verses 21—45, 106th Psalm

On the ceiling is pictured man's confusion in his fears and wicked purposes which led him to abandon the God of Israel for the gods of idolatry. In the lunette the Jews, fallen from the ways of Jehovah, are represented bent in subjection beneath the Assyrians and the Egyptians, beseeching mercy of the Most High, who reaches out from Heaven to lift them up. To appreciate fully, then, Sargent's conception, something of the character and the period of each prophet should be first considered. A few studies are included here, as illustrations of what should be attempted for all.

Moses, founder of the Jewish nation and religion, was prophet, law-giver, writer and historian. Says Graetz: "Amongst all law-givers, founders of states, and teachers of mankind, none has equalled Moses. Not only did he, under the most inauspicious circumstances, transform a horde of slaves into a nation, but he imprinted on it the seal of everlasting existence: he breathed into the national body an immortal soul."

Joshua (Father of His Country) was the hero of the conquest of Canaan, the promised land of Israel. He was the greatest military figure in Hebrew history, and contributed a large share in the building of the Jewish nation. He was loyal, vigorous, masterful, humble, just, brave, unselfish, a devout and a true follower of Jehovah.

Elijah, the prophet of fire, lived in the reign of the idolatrous court of Ahab. He worked to overthrow the Baal-worshipping rulers of his land, succeeded, and thereby saved his country

FRIEZE OF THE PROPHETS.—*Sargent*

Right Center

in a great crisis. He was an austere man; practised self-denial, lived frugally, scorned luxury and ease, and tolerated no frivolity. His courage, steadfastness, loyalty and devotion to God, together with his many achievements gained for him his people's respect and confidence.

2. **Setting.** Sargent Hall, on the third floor of the library building, is eighty-five feet long, twenty-three feet wide and twenty-six feet high. The vaulted ceiling rests upon plain piers which divide the walls into broad panels. Above the Amherst stone wainscoting, the frieze, lunette and ceiling sections are decorated with Sargent's painting. The frieze is made up of five panels, all excepting the central one containing four figures each. The central figure of the central frieze, Moses, is modeled in relief, an unusual departure in mural painting. He is portrayed in a conventional manner wholly unlike the others of the frieze. Why? What is the effect of the formal folds of his robe in contrast with the flowing mantles of the others, and the conventional wings of the Spirit enfolding him. Note the effect of the column-like figures of Elijah and Joshua on either side supporting him. Observe the effect of the costumes of the men in giving an impression of continuity and rhythm. What is the impression conveyed by the stone tablets, the inscriptions on the scrolls carried by Daniel and Jonah?

3. **Arrangement.** There are two striking features of the frieze as a whole which contribute to its appreciation and enjoyment. First, the idea or meaning of the subject is clearly apparent, and second, each individual reveals his inmost thoughts true to his character as indicated in the Biblical account. As has been noted, the figure of Moses, executed in relief, stands out with sculpturesque boldness. Note the preponderance of the heavy vertical lines in the central panel, contributing to the impression of dignity and strength. In the strong figure of Joshua there is a warm, life-like, virile quality which is altogether lacking in the conventional portrayal of Moses. The strong vertical lines are significant of vigor and firmness, as well as of dignity and majesty.

It is interesting to note how effectively the artist has

FRIEZE OF THE PROPHETS.—*Sargent*

Extreme Left

avoided any impression of monotony in the nineteen figures of the frieze. This is quite a problem in itself. Variety must be secured, but it must not come at the expense of unity in a truly great work of art. Elijah and Joshua are excellent examples of the painter's care to avoid repetition. The lines of Joshua's figure are strictly vertical and horizontal; those of Elijah's are in the main curved and suggest the letter S. What is the significance of the lines? Joshua's right arm crosses his chest and unsheathes his sword point downward; Elijah's left arm reaches to the left, where his staff, clasped in his right hand, points upward. Joshua's head is covered, his face averted and shaded; Elijah's head is uncovered, his face uplifted and lighted. Which of the two is the more emotional, the more indicative of the military man, the more self-controlled and the more self-reliant?

Carry the contrast to other figures. The most despairing of the groups on the extreme left is contrasted with the most hopeful one on the extreme right. A pleasing touch balances the abject woe of one group with a prophet of hope, Hosea; the calm faith of the other with a prophet of despair. Note other characteristic positions. Jeremiah, the lonely man, draws apart in mournful, dejected meditation in contrast with the upturned face and sweeping gesture of the questioning Isaiah. Obadiah, the most abject picture of woe one cares to see in a whole lifetime, tears his gray locks in the agony of spirit, while Zephaniah, of quieter mien, holds his aching head in his hands. Joel hides his face in his mantle.

4. **Supreme Motive.** Sargent, above all other things, painted his impression, and painted it strongly, clearly and directly. Intense feeling, whether of despair or of hope, is here shown with varying shades. Behind this show of feeling, however, there is apparent the single, dominating motive of all these men; the bringing of a wayward, sinful nation back to the recognition and worship of the one true, omnipotent Father of men. The conception is a mighty one. It deals with the most exalted ideals of the greatest leaders the race ever produced. It brings into play the strongest emotions of great souls. "I heard the voice of the Lord, saying, Whom shall

FRIEZE OF THE PROPHETS.—*Sargent*
Extreme Right

I send, and who will go for us? Then said I, Here am I, send me.''

''Then the Lord put forth his hand, and touched my mouth and the Lord said unto me, Behold, I have put my words in thy mouth.''

This was the call the prophets heard. Sargent in such a conception, to accomplish a truly great work of art, must make one feel the bigness of such a call to these men. It requires that he paint frankly and with perfect understanding. He must represent statesmen who were instrumental in building a nation. He must reveal the innermost workings of the minds of men, divinely called, who employed the most scathing words of censure, rebuke, denunciation, ridicule and warning in their endeavor to turn their people from the worship of the gods of Baal. He must deal with men who in their forceful sermons and prophecies exhausted literary forms and figures. In a word, he must represent great religious teachers and leaders who above all were true followers of God and who communed with Him from the mountain peaks of spiritual ideals.

Such was the task, and Sargent, vigorous and brilliant, was equal to it.

In the painting of these eighteen figures, Mr. Sargent is entirely the brilliant painter. . . . They are each drawn with an individuality strikingly suggestive of the characters in the Scriptural narrative, and, with their simple draperies thrown about them, stand with the solemnity of a chorus in a classic drama.—King

5. **History.** Sargent was commissioned by the trustees of the Boston Public Library, 1890 to decorate both end walls of the third floor gallery. He received for this work $15,000. Part of the decoration was exhibited, 1894, in the Royal Academy, London. In 1895 the painting was put in place in the library. The work was so satisfactory that an additional $15,000 was raised by popular subscription to enable the painter to unite the decorations of the end walls in a scheme which should include the entire gallery.

QUESTIONS

What is the idea expressed? What, do you think, was the supreme motive of the painter in this frieze? Did he aim for mere decorative effect, or did he seek to give expression to his feeling about the subject? Where is the central group? The central figure? How does the treatment of Moses differ from that of the others? What is the effect of this? What are the impressive details of his figure? Is the impression of the frieze as a whole a definite one? The painting has been compared to a Greek chorus "interpreting and supporting the movement of a great drama." Is the comparison clear? What are the qualities of the painting that would call forth this tribute? What are the striking details of the frieze? Is there variety in the expressions of the individual men? To what extent? What seems to be the dominant feeling running through the entire group? Can you select the leading characters? What are the pleasing features of the arrangement? Could you suggest a different arrangement that might be more effective? Make a character study of the men from their expressions, gestures and positions. Is there a definite indication that Sargent appreciated fully the function and leadership qualities of the prophet? Determine the individuals that express majesty, determination, courage, profound meditation, hopeful mien, fiery resolve, agony of spirit, majestic grief, calm or hope, assurance, simple dignity. Which is the most dramatic group? The most forceful? Contrast Hosea and Zephaniah, Joel and Isaiah, Elijah and Joshua, Jeremiah and Daniel, Obadiah and Zechariah. Compare Moses and Haggai, etc.

THE ARTIST

Sargent, John Singer (1856—), an American artist, was born in Florence, Italy. He was the son of wealthy, cultured parents. While a youth he took a classical course in Florence, where he also became a pupil in the Academy. Later he studied with Carolus Duran in Paris, and assisted him in deco-

rating the Luxembourg. Sargent made an exhaustive study
of the works of the great masters and gained distinction before
he reached middle age. He was awarded the grand prize at
the International Exposition of 1889, 1900.

He is a member of the National Academy of Design, the
Society of American Artists, the Royal Academy and other
art and learned societies. Sargent is best known as a portrait
and figure painter. His best known works in the United States
are the portraits of Edwin Booth, Lawrence Barrett and
Joseph Jefferson, which he painted for the Players Club, New
York; the portraits of ex-President Roosevelt and Secretary
Hay, and the decorations in Sargent Hall of the Boston Public
Library.

Sargent like other artists paints his impression, and he paints it more
frankly and directly than many, with less brooding and less searching for
subtleties—paints it strongly and without reservation; and he leaves the
psychology to those who shall look at his picture.—Cox

THE MINUTE MAN

French

Their feet had trodden peaceful ways;
They loved not strife, they dreaded pain;
They saw not, what to us is plain,
That God would make man's wrath his praise.

No seers were they, but simple men;
Its vast results the future hid:
The meaning of the work they did
Was strange and dark and doubtful then.

—Whittier, *Lexington*

You are set apart,—and forever,—for the esteem and gratitude of the human race.—Emerson

THE STATUE

The minute men were militia authorized by the Province of Massachusetts just before the breaking out of the Revolutionary War. The members of the organization pursued their ordinary vocations, but agreed to respond to the call to arms at a minute's notice.

The minute men constituted the patriot army that confronted the British troops at Lexington and Concord in 1775, and fought the first battle of the "War for Independence."

When the oppression of the mother country could no longer be endured, and when England must be notified that her American colonies had reached the limit of their endurance, the resolution of the Continental Congress, notifying George III that such a limit had been reached, was most welcome news to the people of the colonies. Everyone felt that open war must come. Men everywhere began to prepare for it. It was certain that Massachusetts would become the first battleground.

At Concord the colonists had gathered a quantity of ammunition and supplies, which the British general, Gage, determined to destroy. Eight hundred British regulars were sent out at night from Boston on a secret march to take charge of the stores.

But Paul Revere and some other patriots in Boston had learned of the plan, and Revere, in a daring ride through Middlesex county, warned the minute men of the approach of the British. This ride has been immortalized by Longfellow in his poem *Paul Revere's Ride.*

> A shape in the moonlight, a bulk in the dark,
> And beneath, from the pebbles, in passing, a spark
> Struck out by a steed flying fearless and fleet;
> That was all! and yet, through the gloom and the light,
> The fate of a nation was riding that night.
> And the spark struck out by that steed in his flight
> Kindled the land into flame with its heat.

At Lexington the British regulars, resplendent in their red uniforms, were met by a little band of minute men under the command of Captain Parker, who, on the approach of the British troops, gave this order:

"Stand your ground; don't fire unless fired upon. But if they mean to have war, let it begin here."

The British commander, Major Pitcairn, rode up to the minute men and cried: "Disperse, ye rebels, disperse."

Since no one paid any attention to this command, Major Pitcairn ordered his troops to fire, and the war had begun.

The minute men were obliged to retreat, and the British force marched on to Concord. But the news of their approach had been sent over the county, and without exception the farmers hurried to Concord, where

> By the rude bridge that arched the flood,
> Their flag to April's breeze unfurled;
> Here once the embattled farmers stood,
> And fired the shot heard round the world.
>> —Emerson, *The Concord Hymn*

From the story of this battle, Daniel Chester French, the American sculptor, gained his true conception of *The Minute*

THE MINUTE MAN.—*French*

Man. On the first battlefield of the "War for Independence," one hundred years having passed away, over fifty thousand Americans gathered about this statue. Here, on the same spot where the militia had defended the old bridge, *The Minute Man* was unveiled to the memory of those of whom Emerson said:

They did not know it was a deed of fame they were doing. These men did not babble of glory. They supposed they had a right to their corn and their cattle, without paying tribute to any but their own governors.

As a symbol of true Americanism, *The Minute Man* must appeal to all. How true to life he stands. In rapt attention his eyes scan the distant fields. So alert is he that we seem to listen with him to the drum beats and the alarm bells in the distance. His sleeves are rolled up, revealing the muscular arms, for he has been working in the fields.

Courage and strength are in the upright figure. The head is thrown proudly back. We are led to feel by his own spirited attitude the great responsibility of his position.

We share with him the warlike spirit of independence, for we realize as did the minute men of old the principles involved in that struggle. There is only admiration felt for this stalwart man of dignity and action.

Let the tale be repeated from father to son till all its thrilling incidents are as familiar as household words; and till the names of the brave men who reaped the bloody honors of the 19th of April, 1775, are as well known to us as the names of those who form the circle at our firesides.

—Edward Everett

PLAN FOR STUDY

Source of Subject. The minute man described on the preceding pages.

2. **Setting.** Two monuments mark the scene of the battle at the "Old North Bridge." One, the *Battle Monument,* erected in 1836, marks the British position on the Concord side, the other, *The Minute Man,* stands on the Lexington side of the bridge and marks the American position. Nature's setting for the monuments is ideal. The tranquil river, the picturesque

bridge which spans it, the willow hedge enclosing the spot, the road approaching the bridge on either side, winding through rows of trees, give a charm to the place that once seen is never forgotten. Standing near the *Battle Monument* one can look across the old bridge to the opposite bank, where in plain view is *The Minute Man.*

The bridge is an exact reproduction of the original battle bridge and was dedicated in the same year that witnessed the completion of Mr. French's statue, which stands scarcely a hundred feet from the bridge near the spot where Captain Davis is said to have been fatally wounded. A short distance down the road is the vine-covered cottage where Mr. French worked.

Here beneath the hills they trod, by the peaceful river on whose shores they dwelt, amidst the fields that they sowed and reaped, proudly recalling their virtue and valor, we come to tell their story, to try ourselves by their lofty standard, to know if we are their worthy children.

—George William Curtis

3. **Arrangement.** The figure of *The Minute Man,* crowning a granite pedestal, faces the bridge, dauntless and alert, as though on the opposite shore the British regulars were even now drawn up. The observer is at once impressed by the effectiveness of such an arrangement. The rough, homespun garb of the farmer-patriot speaks plainly of the spirit that caused the plow to be left in the furrow and the musket to be seized at the first note of the alarm.

The undaunted, fearless spirit of the man is revealed in every muscle of his body. His coat is soil-stained, worn and heavy with the "forty charges" of a James Hayward; home-made gaiters encase the sturdy limbs, while in the heat of expected battle his collar is unbuttoned and thrown back. Somehow this costume is very becoming to the volunteer militiamen—so much so that we would not have it changed— no, not for a flashing military uniform. It speaks not of the vainglory on a battlefield, but of some great principle at stake, for which he will drop the work of the fields.

Somehow we feel that the sculptor has breathed into this figure more than a mere individuality. The *Minute Man* is a type. In him we see a nation of freemen, a great principle at stake. This is *the* minute man of the Revolution, inspired by the purest motives to battle and to sacrifice.

> No Berserk thirst of blood had they,
> No battle-joy was theirs, who set
> Against the alien bayonet
> Their homespun breasts in that old day.
>
> —Whittier

The slanting line of the musket gives a sense of forward motion to the body. The predominance of the vertical lines and the height of the pedestal as compared to its width lend dignity to the figure. The collar thrown back discloses the tense muscles of the neck, the rolled-up sleeves reveal the muscular arms, while the tightly laced gaiters show to advantage the clean-cut, sturdy limbs. The plow serves to emphasize the peacefulness of his usual calling, the suddenness with which he has received the summons, and his promptness in assuming the soldier's responsibility.

A finer example of the effectiveness of the minute men's organization could scarcely be conceived. The sculptor chose to portray the fiery spirit of youth. The face is clean-cut and handsome, its drawn muscles bespeak the strength and seriousness of the purpose which is inspiring him.

4. **Supreme Motive.** See pages 237, 238.

5. **Center of Interest.** Our interest centers on the idea which the statue represents.

> So, in the life of nations, there are all-important junctures when the fate of centuries is crowded into a narrow space,—suspended on the results of an hour.—Edward Everett

> Swift as their summons came, they left
> The plow mid-furrow standing still,
>
> .   .   .   .   .
>
> Their death-shot shook the feudal tower,
> And shattered slavery's chain as well;
> On the sky's dome, as on a bell,
> Its echo struck the world's great hour.
>
> —Whittier

6. History. *The Minute Man,* as well as the structure which now spans the Concord river, was erected largely through the efforts of Ebenezer Hubbard, who lived in a century-old homestead a few rods from the historical spot. From his earliest remembrance, the old gentleman had cherished a desire to have the scene of the Lexington conflict marked by a worthy memorial. For many years he laid away part of his earnings, and at his death, in 1870, it was found that he had bequeathed a sufficient sum for a monument. Largely through the efforts of Ralph Waldo Emerson, whose grandfather, Reverend William Emerson, had taken an active part in the Lexington struggle, the commission to model a statue was given to Daniel Chester French, then twenty-two years old. For this work Mr. French received $1,000. The metal for the statue came from ten pieces of brass cannon donated by Congress. The granite pedestal is a part of the same block from which the Battle Monument was hewn.

The statue was unveiled at Concord, Massachusetts, April 19, 1875, the centennial celebration of the Battle of Concord. The occasion was one of national note. President Grant, the members of his cabinet, the Vice-President, the Governor and executive committee of Massachusetts, the Massachusetts Supreme Court, the Legislature, several governors of other states and a number of other prominent men were present. The program included an address by President Grant, and one by Mr. Emerson. James Russell Lowell read a poem for the occasion, and George William Curtis delivered the principal oration.

QUESTIONS

What does this statue commemorate? How was the artist especially fitted for this work? What qualifications for military service do you think the minute men of 1775 possessed? For what principle did they struggle? Why were they called minute men? What was the importance of their struggle at Lexington? What qualities of manly beauty do you note in the statue? Is the minute man young or old? What does the pedestal contribute to the general impression of the statue?

What lines predominate in the statue? What is their effect? Are you pleased with the garb of the man? What does it tell you about his occupation? His duty as a minute man? What idea does the plow add? What would be the effect if it were left out? Of what does the man seem thinking? What does his poise suggest? What details contribute to the general qualities of strength? of resolve? of alertness? of dignity? of courage? of confidence? of action? What supreme attribute of the minute man should always be remembered? What central thought does the sculptor seem to give in his statue? In what ways is his conception of the patriots of old pleasing to you? What do you like best about the figure?

THE SCULPTOR

French, Daniel Chester (1850—), an American sculptor, was born at Exeter, N. H. His father was a judge in the New Hampshire courts. French studied at the Massachusetts Institute of Technology with J. Q. A. Ward, and with Thomas Ball in Florence, Italy. Returning to America, he finally settled in New York. He is one of the foremost of American sculptors. He designed the bronze doors for the Boston Public Library, and became widely known through his colossal gilded statue of the *Republic* for the World's Columbian Exposition in Chicago.

Yet, if it is only on rare occasions that French's work evinces style, it is never without a very rare and fine distinction—the impress of a man who reverences his art and has yielded her the devotion of a refined and elevated spirit. . . . If it fails to touch the deeper chords of human emotion, it is always purifying and uplifting. With maturity it has lost nothing of its original freshness, and has had an abiding influence for good upon American art and life.—Caffin

THE SINGING BOYS

Donatello

THE FRIEZE

Did cold white marble ever mold itself into such grace and life except by a master's touch? Could artist ever put into any theme this perfect maze of childish movement unless he knew every joy, every sorrow, in a word, every impulse of childhood?

A host of children, the freshest, chubbiest, happiest children imaginable, dancing and frolicking, swinging and whirling, shouting and carolling, rush along a bright golden pathway circling the dizzy heights in the mellow glow of the organ loft. What a wealth of expressions their bright faces give. What movement. What joy. What music.

From the fields and woods, from the streets, from humble homes and palaces and from the very portals of the temple, the sculptor has gathered this band of choristers. The freshness and grace and beauty of the Cupid type combined with the rustic vigor of the open country greet us with astonishing reality.

The most enthusiastic shout in joyful ecstacy. Others, seemingly lost in the frolic, look at us with eyes that see not, for their souls have been lifted by the music far away from earthly thoughts. Everywhere the lines teem with movement. Children, carefree, have abandoned themselves to the dance and to music. Like the parts of some great wheel they revolve in unity and grace.

What splendid modeling. How boldly the sculptor has rounded the sturdy limbs and arms, and how true are their lithe active bodies in their flowing marble drapery.

243

PLAN FOR STUDY

1. Source of Subject. Donatello received a commission for a frieze to adorn the organ loft in the Cathedral of Florence. He had learned to mold human figures that were anatomically perfect, but this did not satisfy him. His figures must not only be perfect, they must also have life. Thus, when he had mastered the human figure, it became to him a medium through which he might give that other essential of art—some strong feeling or emotion. A fine opportunity for such an expression came in this commission. It required first of all a theme of music and joy. The closest study of healthy, active children had to be made. He supplemented this study with impressions he had gained from a study of the Cupids of the old Greek and Roman sculptors.

2. Setting. This cantoria or singing gallery was originally designed for a place over a door of the sacristy in the Cathedral of Florence. The gallery today is not as the artist completed it, for in its removal to the museum many beautiful accessories were lost, but the beauty of the cantoria has not been seriously impaired. The frieze is supported by a row of five brackets, beautifully carved. In each of the outer spaces between them two little figures are in action. Above is the gallery itself, with five pairs of pillars supporting a cornice in which are carved alternate urns and acanthus leaves. Arrayed against a mosaic background just within the row of pillars is the group of merry, singing boys. The effect of the entire gallery is very pleasing. The brackets are massive, the pillars, while not large, add much to the simple dignity of the frieze.

The realistic effect gained in arranging the children behind the pillars is noticeable, especially when compared with a similar frieze by Luca della Robbia in the same museum. While one is inclined to think that the pillars mar the continuity of the action, another asserts that they contribute much to the naturalistic effect. The influence of Greek art and architecture is seen in the general architectural plan as well as in the dec-

THE SINGING BOYS.—*Donatello*

orative forms of the urn, the acanthus leaf and the background
of mosaic.

3. **Arrangement.** As noted in the setting, the group of singing children is arranged just behind the row of pillars which
support the cornice. Our illustration shows one section of the
frieze so the pillars do not appear. The group are dancing in
the wildest sort of frolic. Some are boisterous, others, just
brim full of happiness, are content merely to watch their mates,
and all are wholly absorbed in their play. Their faces are not
necessarily pretty. They are just the children the sculptor was
wont to meet in his daily walks through Florence.

The style of relief here employed by Donatello is one that is peculiar to
himself; the figures, although modeled on the surface but slightly and
with the utmost delicacy, stand out in high relief from the background,
for their outline, instead of being rounded to meet it as is usual in bas-
relief sculpture, projects with almost square-cut edges from the ground,
thus securing by means of emphatic and effective shadows the boldness
necessary to a work which is seen from a distance.—Selected

4. **Light and Color.** Seen in the dim light of the sacristy,
the figures of the frieze, almost rough in their outlines, appeared to far greater advantage. Donatello was guided in
making the frieze by the light which it would receive from the
loft. His judgment was correct; the figures modeled so boldly
undoubtedly stood out with much force and beauty. The color
scheme is especially beautiful. The mosaic background is
checkered gold and blue enamel, and the same design and
coloring relieve the pillars.

5. **Supreme Motive.** It is as if the sculptor, inspired by the
strongest love for children, chiseled their joyous frolic to the
strains of beautiful music

> Of voices sweet entuned and so small
> That methought it the sweetest melody
> That ever I heard in my life.   —Chaucer

The function of the cantoria is a melodious one. The sculptor's motive was to fill it with the three most appealing factors

of childhood, music, color and action. There is infinite vitality to their movement which in itself is a theme of beauty.

6. **History.** The frieze was begun in 1433 and was set in place over one of the doors of the sacristy in 1439. In 1688, after art in Italy had suffered its greatest decline, the gallery was torn down and we are told a wooden gallery more to the public taste was built in its place. For many years the frieze lay neglected in the office of the Cathedral Board of Works, where at times it was shorn of various ornamental pieces In 1883, after as many of the accessories as possible had been recovered, the work was transferred to the museum of the Cathedral where Signe del Moro, the architect, restored the Singing Gallery as completely as he was able.

QUESTIONS

What are these children doing? How many do you see? What is the expression on their faces? Is it the same for every one? Of what do the children seem to be thinking? Are all of them thinking of the same thing? What traits of character are revealed in the different faces? What feeling seems to be the same in every one? Do they all show their joy in the same way? Point out as many different attitudes as you can. Which are boisterous? Serene? Brimful of happiness? Composed and quiet, yet full of joy? Devout and full of praise? Purely fun-loving? Most active? In which are you most interested? Why? What is a cantoria? What is a frieze? Where was this frieze first placed? What one feeling should it give in such a place? What are its most beautiful points? What seems to be its chief quality? How is the feeling of movement given? Of song? Of joy? What traits of character are revealed in most of the faces? What are the beautiful qualities of their little forms? What do you like best about the frieze? Does it tell us anything about the sculptor?

THE ARTIST

Don''atel'lo, or **Donato,** *Do nah'to* (about 1386-1466), was an Italian sculptor of the Florentine School, and the foremost sculptor of the early Renaissance. His father, Niccolo di Betto Bordi, was a wool comber. Donatello began his career as an apprentice to a goldsmith. Later he worked for a short time in the studio of Ghiberti and in 1402 went to Rome with Brunelleschi, where he studied the remains of classic art. This sojourn in Rome had a lasting influence upon Donatello, and through him on modern sculpture, of which he is generally considered the founder. He is also credited with preparing the way for Michelangelo.

Donatello was one of the most prolific sculptors of the Renaissance, and his works are in the National Museum and the Duomo, Florence, and in Naples and Peoto. Chief among his works are *St. Peter, St. Mark* and *St. George.*

DAVID

Michelangelo

Bend now thy body to the common weight:
But oh, that vine-clad head, those limbs of morn!
Those proud young shoulders, I myself made straight!
How shall ye wear the yoke that must be worn?

—Margaret Steele Anderson

What a piece of work is man! how noble in reason! how
infinite in faculty! in form and moving how express and admirable!
in action how like an angel!

—Shakespeare

THE STATUE

A mighty throng, the hosts of Israel and Philistia, swaying
and surging like the billows of a great ocean, covered opposite
mountains in battle array.

Forty days had come and gone and their positions remained
unchanged. Between them a broad plain lay unbroken save
only for a brook which murmured its song undisturbed.

A mysterious silence had settled over the armies. Suddenly
a shout rang from the camp of the Philistines. A huge giant
stalked out from their midst and advanced to the middle of
the plain. A cloak of armor clothed his great body, and upon
his head was a helmet of brass.

"Choose a man for you," cried he, "and let him come to me.
If he be able to fight with me and to kill me, we will be your
servants, but if I prevail against him and kill him, then shall
ye be our servants and serve us."

A wail of anguish was the answer of the men of Israel.
How despairing was their cry, their call for a champion!

249

Meanwhile in their midst, a lad was pushing his way to the front.

He was a valiant youth, and his face, like the face of the morning
Gladdened the earth with its light, and ripened thought into action.

For David, youngest son of Jesse, had heard the giant's challenge.

"Who is this Philistine that he should defy the armies of the living God?" he asked of the nearest men.

"Have ye seen this man that is come up? Surely to defy Israel is he come up," said they, "and it shall be that the man who killeth him, the king will enrich him with great riches, and will give him his daughter, and make his father's house free in Israel."

Saul heard of David's arrival, and quickly summoned the lad before him. Astonished, he heard the youth's offer to meet the giant. "Thou art not able to go against this Philistine to fight with him," the king warned, "for thou art but a youth, and he a man of war from his youth."

David, undaunted, replied: "Thy servant kept his father's sheep, and there came a lion, and a bear, and took a lamb out of the flock: and I went after him and smote him, and delivered it out of his mouth: and when he arose against me, I caught him by his beard, and smote him, and slew him. Thy servant slew both the lion and the bear. . . . The Lord that delivered me out of the paw of the lion, and out of the paw of the bear, he will deliver me out of the hand of this Philistine."

Then was Saul convinced. "Go and the Lord be with thee," he directed, and offered David his armor. But the shepherd boy wanted no such restraint. He quietly laid it aside, and grasping his strong staff, ran nimbly to the brook, where he selected five smooth stones and placed them in his bag.

A breathless quiet held the armies. "And when the Philistine looked about, and saw David, he disdained him: for he was but a youth, and ruddy, and of a fair countenance. And the Philistine said unto David, Am I a dog, that thou comest to me with staves? . . . Come to me, and I will give thy flesh unto the fowls of the air, and to the beasts of the field.

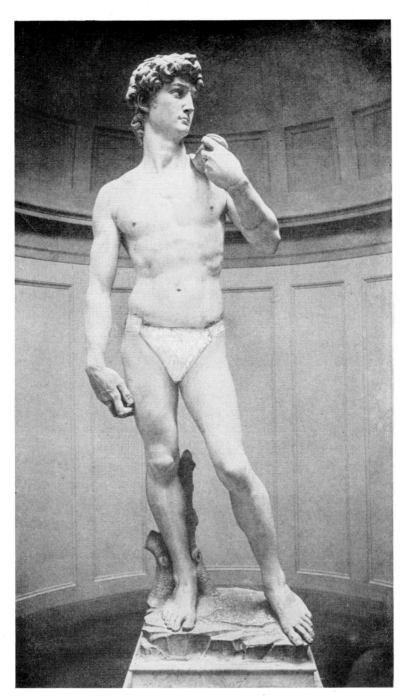

DAVID.—*Michelangelo*

"Then said David to the Philistine, Thou comest to me with a sword, and with a spear, and with a shield; but I come to thee in the name of the Lord of hosts, the God of the armies of Israel, whom thou hast defied."

Before the scornful Goliath the boy, strong, comely and valiant, paused but for a moment. Then gracefully his lithe body bent. His right hand shot far out and up. Whirling and glistening, the stone sped straight to the mark. Full in the forehead it struck the giant and he fell. In terror and dismay the Philistines fled, while David, the shepherd lad, stood victorious.

Did mallet and chisel ever model a figure of more perfect health and vigor? With what skill the sculptor has caught the dauntless lad in a moment of supreme endeavor. Only for an instant does he pause. His clear gaze is taking unerring aim. There is absolute confidence in his bearing, something indescribable which seems to say, "Am I not the anointed of the Lord?"

Keenly he searches the giant's armor. Skilfully he has inserted the pebble in his sling. In his mind, we may be sure, there enters no thought of failure. Had he not often slung at a mark and hit it? Now his muscles become tense, his brow contracted, his eyes grow brighter as he braces his body for a supreme effort. The next instant he will bend. It is as if we might see the quick outreaching movement of the arm which will send the pebble whirling to the mark. Who can calculate the strength of those powerful hands when wielded in the cause of right? Hands that in one moment drew exquisite music from harpstrings, and in the next smote the bearded lion at a single blow.

In the knitted brow, quivering nostrils and straining muscles of the neck is suggested the intense excitement under which he is laboring. Purpose, power and faith, all are mirrored in the resolute features.

> To that dauntless temper of his mind
> He hath a wisdom that doth guide his valor
> To act in safety.

PLAN FOR STUDY

1. **Source of Subject.** In First Samuel, chapter xviii, is to be found the story of David's conquest of Goliath, from which the sculptor drew his conception. David, the seventh and youngest son of Jesse of the tribe of Judah, was born at Bethlehem. His boyhood was spent among the hills of Judea with his flock. Here at eighteen he was secretly anointed king of Israel by the prophet Samuel. His name "beloved one" is significant of the place he held in his people's hearts.

2. **Setting.** The statue originally guarded the entrance of the Palazzo Vecchio, the first seat of the chief magistrates of Florence, where it was placed at Michelangelo's suggestion. Here it stood for three centuries, exposed to the elements, and yet it suffered comparatively little damage. In 1873 it was removed to the Florentine Academy, where it now occupies a niche in the rotunda. The light streams in from above and shows the work to the best advantage possible in an indoor situation.

3. **Arrangement.** The dominant impression of the figure is that of suggested action. The moment is one in which the youth studies the person of his adversary preparatory to hurling the stone which he holds in the middle of his sling upon his left shoulder. Recognizing in the beginning the motive of the sculptor in the arrangement, any criticism impulsively voiced on the first glance may be disarmed. It is true that the figure is not a type of perfect physical development. The slender body has not yet attained that period in its growth where it is in proportion to the great head, the large hands and joints. As one critic observes, the figure wants at least two years to breach the gap between adolescence and the mature and fully developed man.

The figure rests most of its weight upon one leg and leans a trifle backward in preparation for hurling the stone. So well has the sculptor planned the distribution of the enormous weight (nine tons) that only a comparatively small piece of the block against which the right leg rests is needed for additional support. Note the characteristic attitude for using the sling—the right hand holding the cord, the left, clasping the bulging pebble in the sling which extends round his back.

The technique of the *David* is generally conceded to be remarkable. The realism of the figure is on the first glance startling. Observe the muscles of the hands, of the upraised forearm, and the bones of the thorax and of the joints. Observe, too, the straining muscles of the neck which the half-turned head brings into full play. Strength, sternness, dignity, firmness, confidence, and vigor of mind and body, are the most striking qualities of the statue. Can you determine still others?

4. **Supreme Motive.** It is always interesting to note the comments of those who are inclined to emphasize the undeveloped type of youth represented by the *David*, as a quality which detracts from a complete enjoyment of the statue. Some are inclined to compare the figure unfavorably with the Davids of Donatello and Verrochio, both of which, it is claimed, reveal a more poetic and hence a more pleasing conception. Some even carry the comparison to the famous statues of Greek athletes. And right here we must pause to differentiate carefully between two distinct aims in sculpture as well as in painting.

The sculptor, on the one hand, may choose merely to execute a work that will appeal to the eye, to the sense of enjoyment that comes from the contemplation of a human figure perfectly symmetrical. On the other hand, he may seek to represent the feelings which struggle for expression in his own soul, and thus appeal through his art to our emotions. Greek sculpture represents the first type; the second, is illustrated in this statue.

Michelangelo was a deep thinker, and pondered often and long upon the mystery of life. His own career covered many decades in which he witnessed the rise and fall of his own beloved city, Florence. His was a mighty spirit—his nature was of that depth which permitted of no serenity. Life was very real to him. His art was an everlasting challenge. He worked tirelessly, almost feverishly, and his spirit even chafed at times when his own masterful hands seemed incapable of responding to the sublimity of his conception.

Michelangelo has never been excelled, if equalled, in technical skill and accuracy in representing anatomy, yet he was not primarily concerned with merely representing form. He made technique not an end in itself, but a means of expressing some emotion which had given rise to his conception. To him the representation of the human figure was satisfactory only in so far as it was the tangible expression of his supreme spiritual emotion. In his *David* he has caught in marble not only this instant of vigorous endeavor, but the real spirit of this type of youth as well.

Michelangelo was but twenty-four when he conceived the *David*. He knew the dreams and aspirations of the mentally and physically perfect youth. He was experiencing, even then, the flying goals that ever allure those in the dawn of young manhood. He had accepted this commission in his desire to achieve. Could he not appreciate to the fullest the spirit of the valiant young shepherd of Judea? Under sunny skies his *David* had acquired those, qualities of self-reliance, of control, of fortitude, of courage, of daring and of faith, which stay him so well now in this great hour of need. The supreme moment in his young life has come. The test of the period of training is at hand. Upon the aim of a single stone rests the success or failure of his fatherland. The hand that hurls the pebble must be steady, the strong emotions must be under control, the mind clear, the eye keen and the heart pure. His attitude tells us that his confidence is unwavering, his faith supreme.

5. **History.** The history of the statue begins many years before 1501, when the consuls of the wool-weavers' guild of Florence ordered a block of marble eighteen feet long to be transported from Carrara to Florence. Afterwards they had commissioned one Agostino di Guccio to carve from it a statue of a prophet. After he had blocked it out, they abandoned their idea, and the marble remained in this state in the court of the Cathedral for forty years, when Michelangelo's attention was called to the stone and he offered to execute a statue from it. A commission was granted him by the guild, Angust 16, 1501.

Two years were fixed by the committee for the completion of the statue, for which service they agreed to pay the sculptor six florins each month. They agreed further to pay to the sculptor upon receiving the completed work a sum which might seem to them reasonable compensation, and with a little wax model which he had previously worked out, Michelangelo began his task. It is related that in his intense earnestness he often slept with his clothes on in order to be at his work with no delay on the morrow. He was somewhat delayed by a number of political disorders during the period, but in January, 1504, he notified the guild of the *David's* completion.

In 1527, during a popular uprising, a stone thrown by some one in a mob attacking the palace shattered the left arm. The fragments were carefully collected and were restored to the statue in 1543. As has already been stated, the *David* was removed to the Academy of Florence in 1873. It is said that Michelangelo had so completely utilized the marble that a piece of the original surface is still visible on the head of the figure.

COMMENT

The genius which has given such life to marble converts criticism into wonder and admiration.—Horner

The fondness of sculptors for David as a subject was due to the fact that the Florentines, who had spent so much of their time under tyrants, were captivated by the idea of this stripling freeing his compatriots from Goliath and the Philistines. David stood to them, with Judith, as a champion of liberty.—Lucas

In every aspect of the technique of statue-making, the science shown is remarkable.—Freeman

QUESTIONS

What is the type represented? What are the qualities of this type? How is each emphasized in this figure of the David? What is the most striking thing about the statue? What are the striking details of the face? What alluring qualities do you suppose the David had for Michelangelo? Why? Analyze and account for the expression of the youth. What is the instant pictured? What subsequent action is suggested? Is this suggestion a strong one? What makes it so? Is this a sculpture expressive primarily of beauty of form or of strength and beauty of character? What reason can you give for your answer? What are the attractive features of the David? Are there any features which detract from your complete enjoyment of the work? What? Is your impression a definite one? What is it? The David is said to have qualities of force, of might, of impelling and sudden vigor, of control, of confidence, etc. Do you find evidences of these qualities? Can you determine still others? Is this conception of David thoroughly pleasing to you? Can you suggest another arrangement which might prove more effective? What is the sculptor's supreme motive? Does he make it clear? What qualities of his own character does the work reveal?

THE SCULPTOR

Michelangelo Buonarroti, *Mi-kel-an'je-lō   Bö-ō-när-rō'tē* (1475-1564), an eminent Italian sculptor, painter, architect and poet, was born at Caprese.

"It is only well with me when I have a chisel in my hand," the sculptor wrote to a friend. It may be well said he grew up in the sound of the mallet and chisel, for when but a baby he was placed in the care of a stone-cutter's wife. He was of a noble but poor family of Florence. He entered Ghirlandajo's studio in 1488. Lorenzo de Medici, a wealthy patron of art, became interested in him at this time, and took him into his home. In such an environment he had every opportunity for study and progress. His first great work was exhibited in

1501. Not only as a sculptor was he famed, but as a painter, architect and poet. He was often summoned to Rome to execute commissions for the Pope. During his lifetime he served nine of these rulers in the Vatican. His life was spent chiefly in Florence and Rome. One of his most enduring monuments is the dome of St. Peter's in Rome, which he designed while architect of the Cathedral.

Principal Works. *The Last Judgment,* in the Sistine Chapel, 1512; *the Pieta,* 1598; *Holy Family,* Uffizi Gallery, Florence, 1504.

He used his chisel and his pencil to express not merely beautiful artistic motives, but what he felt and thought about the world in which he had to live: and this world was full of the ruin of republics, the corruption and humiliation of society, the subjection of Italy to strangers. In Michelangelo, the student of both art and history finds an inestimably precious and rare point of contact between the spirit of an age and its external expression in sculpture and painting.—Symonds